Praise For The Covert Passive-Aggressive Narcissist

"The Covert Passive-Aggressive Narcissist belongs on every survivor's bookshelf. Debbie Mirza's book is a compassionate and healing resource for anyone seeking relief after narcissistic abuse. She clearly identifies subtle red flags that are often so difficult for survivors to pinpoint, while also encouraging the reader to look inward for solutions. Her warm and encouraging words are like receiving a written hug when you need it most."

Jackson MacKenzie, author of *Psychopath Free* and *Whole Again*

"This is an insightful book for therapists working with complex trauma and/or Complex-PTSD. Clinicians can diagnose 'textbook' narcissism. However, covert passive-aggressive narcissism is difficult to identify and not widely recognized in the field of mental health therapy. Debbie shines a light on interpersonal relationships with a CPAN by naming experiences and behavioral patterns. As a clinical social worker, I love this book and use it as a basis of understanding clients who have experienced emotional and psychological abuse by someone they love. Thank you for having the wisdom to write this book and validate the invisible scars of survivors because this is where healing begins."

Denise Malm, LSWAIC, GMHS

"The Covert Passive-Aggressive Narcissist brings a massive sigh of relief to people who have been involved with, were raised by, or worked with someone who has made them feel crazy, exhausted, depressed, unworthy, guilty, terrified, and chronically anxious, while they charmed and amazed others. Debbie Mirza provides insight, answers, and healing to those who have wondered whether they have been abused by a narcissist but have not found themselves or their answers in the current literature on narcissist abuse. As a clinical psychologist for over 20 years, I find that **The Covert Passive-Aggressive Narcissist** *fills in the missing pieces in this field for clinicians and victims alike. Debbie clarifies this phenomenon/personality disorder when I have struggled to explain it in my own life and in the stories of countless patients. You aren't crazy: this book helps you identify and name the abuse—so you can be free to truly reclaim your life."*

Dr. Robin LW Alchin Ph.D., Clinical Psychologist, Dana Point, CA

"Passive-aggression. Narcissism. These terms are bandied about in 21st-century America, often without a clear definition, and without understanding how to respond effectively once they are recognized.

Enter Debbie Mirza, and her brilliant, immensely helpful book, **The Covert Passive-Aggressive Narcissist**. She realized that passive-aggression and narcissism coexist, that these behaviors are epidemic in our culture and that millions of people are guilty of them. She realized it because she herself was once the target of a covert passive-aggressive narcissist (CN). After finding her way out, she used her experience to write her book, and, in so doing, she is helping other targets to escape from their base relationships.

Chapter 3 uniquely describes those who are likely to be victimized by CNs: empathic, compassionate, nurturing, trusting, dependable, flexible—all the positive traits of beautiful human beings. Their task is to realize their sense of self-worth in order to extricate themselves from the grip of the CN and to find peace. Debbie's book offers multiple strategies for doing so, including a checklist of Traits of Real Love, so that the survivor recognizes it when it is found.

Clients to whom I have recommended this book have found all or parts of it immediately applicable to their situation. It is a book to be read and re-read by clients and therapists alike, as it is an important contribution to self-help literature."

Dr. Judy M. Sobczak, Ph.D., Licensed Psychologist, private practice, Novi, MI

"As a psychotherapist, this book has proven to be an outstanding, effective tool to help clients in these types of relationships be able to finally understand and clearly know what they are dealing with. The author does an excellent job of clearly identifying and providing a name to all the "crazy-making" behaviors the covert passive-aggressive narcissist does in order to make my clients feel like they are never enough. It identifies those gaslighting behaviors, dissects and defines them one by one, in a clear, concise way with lots of real-life examples. Before I read this book, I didn't have the words to describe a dysfunctional relationship of this sort. Now I do…and it has made a world of difference to my clients by not only improving their lives but also eliminating depression and anxiety symptoms which were a result of the covert passive aggressive narcissist's behaviors."

Pam Hauke, MSW, LCSW, SAC

THE COVERT PASSIVE-AGGRESSIVE NARCISSIST

Recognizing the Traits and Finding Healing After Hidden Emotional and Psychological Abuse

DEBBIE MIRZA

Foreword by Meredith Miller

DebbieMirza.com
Author photograph by Cassie Louthan

ISBN 978-0-9986213-4-0 (paperback)
ISBN 978-0-9986213-5-7 (eBook)

Publisher's Cataloging-In-Publication Data
Prepared by The Donohue Group, Inc.)

Names: Mirza, Debbie, author. | Miller, Meredith, 1978- writer of supplementary textual content.
Title: The covert passive-aggressive narcissist : recognizing the traits and finding healing after hidden emotional and psychological abuse / Debbie Mirza ; foreword by Meredith Miller.
Description: Monument, CO : Safe Place Publishing, [2017] | Includes bibliographical references.
Identifiers: ISBN 9780998621340 (paperback) | ISBN 9780998621357 (ebook)
Subjects: LCSH: Narcissism. | Passive-aggressive personality. | Psychological abuse. | Interpersonal relations. | BISAC: FAMILY & RELATIONSHIPS / Abuse / Domestic Partner Abuse. | PSYCHOLOGY / Psychology / Personality Disorders.
Classification: LCC BF575.N35 M57 2017 (print) | LCC BF575.N35 (ebook) | DDC 158.21--dc23

Printed in the United States

Although the author and publisher have made every effort to ensure that the information in this book was correct at press time, the author and publisher do not assume and hereby disclaim any liability to any party for any loss, damage, or disruption caused by errors or omissions, whether such errors or omissions result from negligence, accident, or any other cause.

This book is not intended as a substitute for the medical advice of physicians. The reader should regularly consult a physician in matters relating to their health and particularly with respect to any symptoms that may require diagnosis or medical attention.

The names and some identifying details shared in this book have been changed to protect the privacy of individuals.

Dedication

To my mom, who was the embodiment of unconditional, tender, authentic love.

You gave me the greatest gift of all.

Thank you.

Table of Contents

Foreword

Three years ago, my reality was imploding all around me like a scene from the movie *Inception*. Everything I had believed to be true was suddenly collapsing. I was forced to face the truth. Until that moment, I couldn't quite put my finger on exactly what the problem was. I was mostly in denial about it, but I think I knew something was wrong for a while.

As one of my friends mentioned the word *narcissist*, she pointed out, *"He's like the ones from the past, he's just the more sophisticated model."*

The heartbreaking dissolution of that relationship sent me on a journey to Peru where I met several more characters like him, mostly in my work life. A year later and totally devastated, I reluctantly went back to the original covert abuser in my life to get on my feet again.

Back where it all began, first the complex-PTSD breakdown happened and then I broke through. Observing my mother with new awareness, I was finally able to see where that pattern of relationships came from. In facing my wound and working on healing, I created a new sense of purpose and the work I do now to help people self-heal after narcissistic abuse.

Recently, when one of my clients told me she was writing a book on covert narcissists, I was so excited that I offered to write the foreword. I'm grateful that Debbie dedicated herself to write this book on such an important, nuanced topic within the genre of narcissistic abuse.

This book is meeting a great need because unfortunately there is not enough information available for people who have been through the more covert forms of abuse. It's incredibly sophisticated and stealth, so it's often missed by mental health professionals who were not trained to recognize it.

Debbie writes,

> *"You think you're on the right track after discovering narcissistic personality disorder, but then you read things that are not completely what you experienced. Coverts do have a grandiose sense of self, are preoccupied with fantasies of power, require excessive admiration, but they hide all these attributes so people will like and trust them."*

She *gets* it. The author clearly knows this war from the front lines.

After years of talking with people in my personal and professional life about covert narcissists, I've come to believe that in order to really understand the nature of the covert narcissist, you have to have lived it. Whether it's a spouse, significant other, friendship, boss, coworker, neighbor, or family member, the patterns are nearly identical and only someone who has been inside that nightmare can really know what the experience is like. Even then it's hard to describe.

I believe the covert types are by far the most dangerous because of their ability to fly stealth, undetected by normal radar. They leverage their intelligence through a meticulous choice of words and silence in order to manipulate others. The smarter the narcissist, the more dangerous because the cloak of invisibility is so high-tech. The overt type of abuser is much more obvious because they lack the intelligence to manipulate as cleverly, so they resort to aggression and violence as their primary weapons.

Plausible deniability is the covert narcissist's greatest weapon in their arsenal of gaslighting tools.

With a covert narcissist everything on the surface looks normal and often lovely for months, years, even decades. They know how to say all the right things, exactly the things that you personally want to hear. They can mirror empathy, concern, and tears better than most Hollywood actors. However, underneath the surface the feeling is off. It's so subtle that you could easily miss it or dismiss it. After a relationship with a covert narcissist, you feel like you can't trust your perception of reality because no one else can see what you see. Most people adore covert narcissists because of how very careful they are in choosing who they unmask around and how much effort they put into optics and public perception.

When you ask for advice from friends and even professionals, you might only hear people giving the benefit of the doubt to the covert narcissist or worse yet telling you that you're being paranoid, overreacting, or some other way of blaming the victim. Unfortunately, asking advice from people who don't understand these high-level tactics can feel invalidating, lead you to more setbacks, and possibly even encourage you to stay in a dangerous situation.

It's terrifying when every part of your intuition is telling you something is really wrong, but the covert narcissist and everyone else are telling you that things are just fine, and implying that maybe you are the problem.

Survivors of covert narcissists need to know they're not crazy. This is the primary concern I hear from clients who were with covert types of abusers. Reading this book will give you that validation.

The recovery of self-trust after abuse by a covert narcissist can take some time. Be patient with yourself in this process. You have been through a severe relational trauma and while you can't see your wounds, they are very real.

This book will help you to understand what happened in your relationship with a covert narcissist through an inventory of their typical characteristics and behaviors, in addition to survivors' stories of interactions with them. You'll likely have many *aha* moments when you connect the dots to similar experiences that happened to you.

I know this book is going to help a lot of people make sense of the insensible.

Big hug to you!

Meredith Miller
Coach & Author
Mexico City, Mexico

Preface

Are you in a romantic relationship or coming out of one that is incredibly confusing and makes you feel like you're going crazy?

Does your mother appear amazing to everyone else, but growing up you felt alone, found it hard to have your own identity, and you felt like things were always your fault?

Did you feel like you walked on eggshells growing up with your dad and still find it hard to connect with him, but people have always told you how lucky you are to have a dad like yours?

Do you have a boss or coworker who everyone thinks is great, but after years of working with them, you find yourself experiencing a lot of anxiety, never feeling good enough, and questioning your own sanity?

Has someone told you your loved one might be a narcissist? You've done some research, but are confused because the person you are wondering about doesn't come across as a self-absorbed, arrogant, over-the-top person who fits the description of a narcissist?

If any of these scenarios resonates, you could be dealing with a covert narcissist. This is the hardest type of narcissist to diagnose because they are so disguised, so covert.

Covert narcissism is the most insidious form of narcissism because the abuse is so hidden. Most people don't even realize they are being abused when they are in these relationships. The life inside them is slowly depleted over time as a result of devaluing tactics by the narcissist. Their self-worth is beaten down. There are no visible scars, but the impact these people have on you is profound.

You have been emotionally and psychologically abused and you are often the only one to see this side of them while everyone around the narcissist thinks they are great. This furthers your confusion and minimizes your pain.

One reason covert narcissists are so damaging is because of cognitive dissonance. This is when you have two competing thoughts in your mind. You love your mom, spouse, boyfriend, or girlfriend and thought they loved you the same. Yet when you look back, their behaviors make you question your beliefs about them. As you reflect, you begin to wonder, *Could this person really have been controlling and manipulating me for years and I didn't see it...or were things really my fault and I'm just overdramatizing my experience?* You have a solid belief that has formed over years that this is a good person who cares about you, and at the same time, they are being incredibly cruel and controlling. The cognitive dissonance is dizzying and crazy-making.

The overt types of narcissists are obvious, in-your-face people. They will let others know how great they are. When their mask comes off, others around them roll their eyes and say, *"Oh, yeah, he's terrible."*

On the other hand, *covert* narcissists tend to be well-liked. They are charming and kind. They appear humble and empathetic.

They can be good listeners and appear to really care. You can feel incredibly loved by them. They simultaneously make you feel terrible about yourself. They use cloaked tactics that you don't see for years.

It is common for people to be in romantic relationships with covert narcissists for more than 10, 20, 30, or even 40 (plus) years and not recognize the abuse they have endured for decades.

This is especially devastating when it is a family member. Sometimes you are the only one who sees it when your siblings still think their dad or mom is amazing and blame you for a plethora of issues. You feel like you must be missing something and you start minimizing the abuse, yourself. If no one else sees it, it must be you who is the problem.

This type of abuse does not look as messy as it really is. It is so invisible it's hard to put your finger on what is wrong.

If you relate to any of this, you are not alone, and you can trust yourself.

I went through years of confusion and cognitive dissonance, myself. I have been involved with several covert narcissists in my life.

Years ago, I searched for answers to help with my own confusion. I read a lot of books on narcissism, but could not find any on the covert type. After years of piecing together information from various sources, I decided to write the book I had needed and couldn't find so other survivors would have the information that would help you heal, all in one place.

In preparation for this book, I interviewed more than 100 survivors. I did in-depth research on the topic because I wanted to make sure this book would be accurate, comprehensive, and incredibly helpful for you. You deserve that.

As I met more and more people who have experienced this type of relationship, my heart was affected tremendously. Witnessing their pain, their wounded hearts, and their strength was humbling and brought out a fierceness in me that made me want to make this the most helpful book I possibly could.

In the following pages, I explain the traits of a covert narcissist. I share lots of stories from people I've interviewed to illustrate the traits. All the names have been changed and details altered so their identities are protected.

I facilitate a support group in my area and have seen how important stories are. When I begin the meetings, I often ask what they are hoping to get out of the evening. Most people say, *"Stories! I need to hear stories so I know I'm not crazy."* You will read plenty of stories in this book to help you recognize things you have experienced and help validate the truth of what you have been through.

I also spend a lot of time talking about healing. If you have read this far, my hunch is you have probably been through or are going through a tremendously difficult and crazy-making experience with a covert narcissist. You deserve to find clarity and ultimately heal the wounds this relationship has caused.

Being with a covert narcissist can take you far away from the person you really are. My hope is this book will help bring you back to your stunning self.

May you find all the answers you are looking for and come to a place of freedom and peace. That may not feel possible right now, but trust me, it is.

With so much love,
Debbie Mirza

Introduction

"Is your husband a narcissist?"

"No! I would never use that word to describe him. He's the nicest guy. Everybody loves him. You would love him if you met him."

"Yes, that's what they are like." The divorce attorney saw Amy's confused face, walked closer to her and said with concern, "I am seeing a lot of classic signs, Amy. I suggest when you get home, you get a hold of as much information as you can about narcissists because you need to know what you're dealing with."

Amy left the appointment in a daze. *Narcissist?* That was the last word she would have used to describe her husband of more than 30 years. She had always seen him as kind, someone she respected. Their relationship wasn't perfect, but most of the time she would have described it as a good marriage. She felt lucky to be with someone so easygoing. However, his behavior over the past year had been vastly different from the man she thought she knew. So many things didn't make sense. The way he was treating her was so hurtful, disturbing, and utterly confusing. Then suddenly, he was done with her. The end of the marriage was shocking and incredibly confusing.

When Amy first met her husband, she felt lucky to have met such a great guy. He was kind. He talked about his feelings. He listened to her, asked her questions about herself, and really wanted to know her. Her family and friends loved him and felt so happy she had met someone like him.

It was remarkable how alike they were. It all felt so easy. The first year they dated was pure bliss. Then things became difficult, but that was because of outside circumstances, Amy always believed. They worked through things. Their communication was great, she thought. They had some issues, but always talked about things. She considered him her best friend.

Recently, though, Amy's husband had been treating her in ways she had never experienced. This man she had seen as kind and loving had become incredibly cruel and aggressive toward her. He was continuously telling her all the things he believed were wrong with her and blaming her for making it impossible for their marriage to work. All of this seemed to come out of nowhere. After 30 years, he moved out and made sure she knew how much happier he was without her. It didn't seem to bother him at all that this was ending. He wanted out, and according to him, it was all her fault.

Amy decided to take her attorney's advice, reading books as well as articles on narcissism, hoping this might be the piece that would finally make sense of this confusing puzzle.

When Amy read the descriptions of narcissists, she kept thinking, *That doesn't sound like him.* Each book described someone who was flashy, drove expensive cars, liked to show off their fancy homes, people who were aggressive, annoying, and obviously self-centered. She read stories of gaslighting that seemed extreme. At the same time, amidst the grandiose images, there were some things that did sound like her husband.

Amy read the basic traits—lack of empathy, rage, lacking a strong sense of self, controlling, manipulative, selfish. She began to feel like her eyes were opening to things she had not seen previously.

Even though Amy believed her marriage was good, she had spent years doubting herself, believing she was to blame for issues that did arise in the marriage. Now, the way she was being treated felt wrong, even though she still wondered if the things he was saying about her were true. He seemed so confident and sounded so rational. His words to her were cruel, but they were also mixed with loving words that made it even more confusing. When she was in conversations with him, her body felt muddled and even nauseated at times. It was hard for her to think clearly. She felt run over and talked down to by him. The words that came out of him were demeaning. He would "teach" her about life and how she needed to be.

Amy found herself calling close friends and family and asking them questions like:

> *"Am I controlling and manipulative like he's saying I am and I just don't see it? Am I inconsiderate? Maybe I have been selfish? I can't think clearly. I can't even see what is true about me anymore."*

Amy needed reminders of who she really was because she felt like she was losing her mind. While she was feeling incredibly emotional and unstable, he was calm and rational, which made her question herself even more.

Amy became a voracious reader about narcissism. She also went to a therapist who was an expert on the subject. The therapist asked odd questions like:

> *"Did your husband forget things a lot, like when you would ask him to pick up some apples while he was at the store?"*
>
> *"Yes! About 70% of the time. When he would go to a coffee shop I would ask if he could get me some water while he was in there. He would happily say 'Sure!' About 7 out of 10 times he would come back to the car with no water and say, 'Oh! I'm so sorry. I totally forgot.' He seemed like he felt bad each time. I would always tell him it was okay. I felt frustrated and confused because it happened so often, but I didn't feel like it was okay for me to be upset because it was an honest mistake. Is this common with narcissists?"*
>
> *"Yes. Very. Did he ever go back and get you water?"*
>
> *"No. Never. I never thought about that."*
>
> *"What about your birthdays?" the therapist asked. "What were those like with him?"*
>
> *"They were awful. But the thing is I can't tell you exactly why." Amy's face scrunched up in confusion. "He wasn't mean to me. He always bought me gifts. Sometimes took me out to dinner. For some reason, though, I ended up crying on my birthdays and apologizing to him for something. I don't even remember why now. Maybe not being appreciative enough? He would buy me things, but many times they were things I didn't want. Then he would tell me a long story about how he found this gift and all the thought and effort that went into it, and I would feel like I needed to have a big reaction even though it was something I never would*

4

have wanted. Then I'd feel bad because I was being shallow and not grateful. Birthdays were always disappointing, and I was glad when they were over. They wore me out for some reason. It never felt like he enjoyed celebrating me, treating me. He always seemed irritated that he had to do things for me. Sometimes he would spend a lot of money and get me something grandiose. It actually stressed me out because of the amount of money he used. I didn't feel like I could say anything because of all the trouble he had gone to."

"When he gave you big things or made grandiose gestures, were other people around to see?"

"Well, when I think about it, yes. Always… That's interesting. I never thought about that. I don't remember any private moments where he would give me something special that showed how well he knew me and how much he loved me. I didn't feel loved on my birthdays, looking back."

With each question, Amy realized she must learn more.

One day, after telling her story to another therapist who had a lot of experience with narcissistic abuse, Amy heard a term she had not seen in her research that changed everything for her. The therapist said, *"It sounds like your husband is a Covert Passive-Aggressive Narcissist. Those are the hardest to recognize."*

Amy felt chills go up her spine. *"Please tell me more about that."*

Everything began to make sense for the first time. Hearing "covert passive-aggressive" in front of the word "narcissist" gave her the missing piece she needed for her quest to understand what was happening. It sent her on a journey that would change her life forever, and ultimately bring her the clarity and healing she so desperately needed and deserved.

Amy now leads men and women through different healing modalities for narcissism in the mountains of Peru and feels tremendously fulfilled and happy. Years ago, when she first discovered the truth of her marriage, she never would have imagined she would someday feel so free and happy. She now has a glow about her that inspires others and gives them hope. She knows who she is and has learned to trust herself implicitly.

Amy was one of the women I interviewed as part of my research for this book. Her story reflects what I heard from so many who have experienced a relationship with a covert narcissist.

If you are reading this, I imagine you might relate to part of Amy's story, maybe even a lot of it. You may be on your own search, trying to make sense of a very confusing person in your life. This book is for you, to give you clarity, strength, and understanding. It will educate you as well as give you hope.

The word "narcissist" is thrown around a lot and grossly misused. *"He's so narcissistic! Oh, yeah, I was with a narcissist too!"* People often use this word to describe someone who is selfish and arrogant. The true definition goes much deeper, and when the word is so carelessly used, it diminishes the painful reality of victims of true narcissists. Someone who has experienced a true narcissist would never toss the word around so lightly.

We tend to label people a lot, and that can be destructive, but in this case, the label is important. When victims are looking for answers and they finally discover their partner or parent or coworker might be a covert narcissist, so many things begin to make sense. It is incredibly helpful in understanding and starting to heal.

I was talking about healing and restoration to one survivor I interviewed. Through tears, she looked at me. Her voice shaking, she asked, *"Do you think it's even possible?"* It is for this woman and so many others like her that I have written this book. Profound healing and freedom are absolutely possible. I, along with so many others, am proof of this. There is hope. The healing you will experience is profound and will bring you to a strong place inside yourself.

Both genders are affected by this destructive personality disorder. I interviewed women and men who have experienced this abuse. Most people I talked to struggled to describe the relationship. There was a perpetual confused look on each face.

This is common. It can be difficult to explain because the abuse is so hidden and subtle. They weren't yelled at or physically abused. There are no visible scars. Yet the impact it makes on the psyche is profound. Like the people I interviewed, I have also experienced covert narcissists (several, actually). I know what it's like to be subtly abused for a long time without recognizing it. I also know what it's like trying to find information on the covert type. You think you are on the right track after discovering narcissistic personality disorder, but then you read things that are not completely what you experienced. You read about aggressive behavior, physical abuse, dramatic stories of deception, and you think maybe you are off track. Your story doesn't appear that bad compared to what you are reading, which then diminishes your own pain and adds to your confusion. That's why I felt it was so important for me to write this book and put everything I had learned into one place.

Many people who go to therapy to get help because they are depressed, low on energy, experiencing low self-esteem, feeling a lot of anxiety, and confused have no idea that the cause of their issue is an abusive relationship, whether that is with a romantic partner, a parent, or someone at work.

Some victims become re-traumatized by a therapist or friend who doesn't understand. Most therapists are not educated about the covert type of narcissism. Only the overt type is taught in higher education, so most don't recognize the signs and traits. I talked to one woman who was in a covert relationship and went to therapy for 10 years. She tried a few different therapists because no one seemed to be able to help her with her depression, anxiety, and lack of energy. They didn't recognize she was in an abusive relationship. Finally, she tried another therapist who after 15 minutes told her she was in an abusive relationship. The others couldn't see it. Neither could she.

This is such a common story. This woman lived for years thinking something was wrong with her. She was being subtly manipulated and devalued at home without seeing it. Her body was reacting. She was slowly dying inside and couldn't figure out why. Thank goodness for the therapist who understood covert narcissism and recognized the signs.

When the relationship ultimately ends in a breakup or divorce, victims have a difficult time understanding what just happened. When a relationship with a covert narcissist ends, it is sudden and painful. It can look like a "normal" divorce, but it is not even close.

Well-meaning friends and family often wonder why it is so hard for you to get past the partner, why you have no desire to date anyone, why it is taking you so long to recover and get back to the way you used to be. Breakups are a part of life, but this type of breakup is a whole other animal. The only people who can fully understand what you are going through are those who have gone through it themselves.

You might be wondering whether you are on the right track when you picked up this book. You may wonder if you are being overly dramatic and looking for someone to blame by thinking your ex or parent or coworker might be a narcissist. Here's the thing: I am sure the narcissist in your life has given you the opposite message about yourself, but the truth is some of the smartest people I've met are people who have been in relationships with covert narcissists.

A helpful thing to notice while you are trying to find answers is the fact that men and women who are with healthy people don't enter words into online search engines such as "toxic relationships"; "energy vampires"; "mean spouses"; "confusing relationships"; "hidden abuse"; "subtle abuse"; "manipulation"; "narcissism"; "covert narcissism"; "sociopaths." The same is true for people who are going through a divorce or a breakup where they just realized they weren't a good match, or they fell out of love, or they find themselves wanting other things. If you are searching for answers because you feel utterly confused, you are on the right track because you're smart. If your body feels weak and flustered around someone, it knows something is not right.

Trust your gut, your intuition, how your body feels. There is nothing wrong with you. You know more than you probably give yourself credit for. You are a brilliant individual who has been beaten down, lied to, and manipulated, so you naturally have a lot of self-doubt. That is normal and completely understandable.

What you have been through is not a small thing. There are several types of narcissists. The covert type is one of the most destructive to your heart, psyche, and physical body because you are usually the only one who sees it. People who know the narcissist in your life probably think they are one of the nicest people they've ever met and often wish they could be as lucky as you to have a mom, husband, dad, wife, boyfriend, boss, or friend like you do.

They feel the same way you did, maybe for a long time, about the covert narcissist in your life. They have witnessed the same illusion, but have not yet identified the truth.

The more my own eyes began to open, the more overwhelming grief and anger I felt. With time, education, and support, this awakening turned into a growing strength and hope inside me. This will happen for you, too. Reading this book is going to be incredibly helpful for you as you begin to awaken to the truth of what you have been through. If you have lived with a covert narcissist, you have been held down for a long time. You have experienced the illusion of love, not the real thing. You have been lied to, manipulated, and controlled. You have not been heard or respected. You were devalued and brutally discarded by someone who said they cared about you, but in fact only cared about themselves. You have experienced an insanity-inducing relationship that is difficult to describe. Your self-confidence, your zest for life, your adventurous spirit, and the light inside you have slowly dimmed. There is a part of you that may not want to be here anymore, but is scared to say that out loud or to anyone else. I understand. I've been there. This is common among survivors.

Here is the good news: you have begun a journey that will bring you to the truth you are seeking, the truth of what you have been through, and the realization of how stunning and valuable you actually are. With time, you will have clarity and feel strength and freedom that may be hard to comprehend right now, but trust me, it's possible. You will experience love (the real thing this time), and you will cherish every moment of it because of what you've been through. Your light will come back brighter than it's ever been. You will be able to love people and help others in ways you couldn't have before. You will be free. Life will actually feel enjoyable, and you'll be glad you're here. I promise you this is all possible.

I spent years researching for my own understanding and healing and have put all the valuable information I learned into one book to make things easier for you. For this book, I decided to dive even deeper by reading more books, finding additional articles, watching more YouTube videos, and interviewing more than 100 people around the world who have experienced a covert narcissistic wife, husband, mother, father, sister, brother, boss, boyfriend, girlfriend, or friend. The interviews were fascinating. Even though our stories differed, and some of the relationship types differed, I felt as if I were looking into a mirror when each person told me their story over Skype or across the table at a restaurant. These brave people furthered my motivation to get all this information down in one place.

I also interviewed therapists and life coaches who specialize in this area. They were extraordinarily helpful, and I will share what I learned from them, as well.

At the end of the book, I include a list of helpful resources for you to further study if you'd like.

This can feel like a lonely road because often you are the only one who ever sees this side of the narcissist. To give you a sense of how not alone you are, here is one statistic:

> *The World Narcissistic Abuse Awareness Day website (www.wnaad.com) estimates "over 158 million people in the U.S. alone are abused by a person with either narcissistic personality disorder or antisocial personality disorder."*

The two have similar traits.

This is a massive problem that seems to be growing. One therapist I interviewed said she didn't know what was happening, but every person who has walked through her door in the past couple years is dealing with narcissistic abuse. Her appointments are constantly booked.

You are definitely not alone.

Meeting the people I've interviewed has made me discover a world out there I didn't know existed. When survivors find each other, there is an immediate connection, a feeling of safety, of understanding. We find ourselves enthusiastically nodding with relief when we hear each other's stories.

My intention for this book is to provide you with a tremendous amount of information, including different things you can do to heal.

I will be using three different terms when referring to a person who has experienced covert narcissistic abuse and would like to explain my thoughts behind them.

If you have been the recipient of this behavior, you were a target and a victim, and you are a survivor. The word "victim" can elicit reactions in people because we are warned against having a "victim mentality." The truth is you were a victim. This doesn't mean that this needs to be a cloud that follows you the rest of your life. You were a person who was harmed. That is the definition of a victim.

You were also a target, as hard as that is to believe and accept. Covert narcissists seek out certain types of people. They look for people who are kind, authentic, self-reflective, nurturing, loving, and caring people with a conscience. They look for energy supplies. Without these attributes, the narcissist has no use for you, as their manipulative tactics wouldn't work.

You are also a survivor. You experienced subtle, manipulative abuse and you are still here. Many people come out of these relationships not wanting to be here anymore after years of being emotionally beaten down. So the fact that you are still here getting up every morning is something to be recognized and commended. You are a survivor. You are stronger than you know.

My hope is this book will bring you the clarity and understanding you want and need.

Welcome to the beginning of your freedom.

1
What is a Covert Passive-Aggressive Narcissist?

There are several types of narcissists. If you search for "types of narcissists" on the Internet, you will find countless articles listing many types and subtypes. Some are classified as overt, covert, somatic, cerebral, parasitic, and boomerang. All narcissists have the same core traits. The official list of these traits is found in the *Diagnostic and Statistical Manual of Mental Disorders, Fourth Edition* (DSM-IV). Mental health professionals use this manual when diagnosing patients.

According to the DSM-IV, a patient must have at least five of the following traits to be diagnosed as having narcissistic personality disorder:

A pervasive pattern of grandiosity (in fantasy or behavior), need for admiration, and lack of empathy, beginning by early adulthood and present in a variety of contexts, as indicated by five (or more) of the following:

   1. Has a grandiose sense of self-importance (e.g., exaggerates achievements and talents, expects to

be recognized as superior without commensurate achievements).

2. Is preoccupied with fantasies of unlimited success, power, brilliance, beauty, or ideal love.

3. Believes that he or she is "special" and unique and can only be understood by, or should associate with, other special or high-status people (or institutions).

4. Requires excessive admiration.

5. Has a sense of entitlement (i.e., unreasonable expectations of especially favorable treatment or automatic compliance with his or her expectations).

6. Is interpersonally exploitative (i.e., takes advantage of others to achieve his or her own ends).

7. Lacks empathy; is unwilling to recognize or identify with the feelings and needs of others.

8. Is often envious of others or believes that others are envious of him or her.

9. Shows arrogant, haughty behaviors or attitudes.

What are your thoughts after reading this? You might look at these and see how they fit perfectly the person in your life who you think may be a narcissist. Perhaps you feel confused because this list doesn't exactly sound like the person you're trying to figure out. Maybe one or two traits match. If it doesn't quite match or only matches a few, the person either isn't a narcissist or is a covert narcissist (CN).

The word *"covert"* is defined in the Merriam-Webster Dictionary as *"not openly shown."* *"Passive-aggressive"* is defined as *"displaying behavior characterized by the expression of negative feelings, resentment, and aggression in an unassertive passive way."*

The narcissistic traits are true of overts and coverts. The difference is the covert narcissist hides their dark attributes because they want people to like them. Their reputation is extremely important to them. Overt narcissists are usually annoying people. Most people don't like them. They are showy. They love to talk about their achievements. It is obvious they are all about themselves. The overt narcissist is the type of person who will go on and on about how great they are, how much they've accomplished while people in the room listening are rolling their eyes.

Overt narcissists tend to have shorter marriages and romantic relationships. It is common for people to be married to coverts for decades and not know they are married to one for most of the relationship. It is also common for people to be in dating relationships with covert narcissists (CNs) that go on for years. Children of covertly narcissistic parents often do not realize the truth about their mom or dad until their thirties.

Covert narcissists will often have careers that are impressive. They can be pastors, spiritual leaders, therapists, and heads of non-profit organizations. They can be politicians who are charming, look you right in the eye, and really seem to care. Coverts do have a grandiose sense of self, are preoccupied with fantasies of power, require excessive admiration, but they hide these attributes so people will like and trust them. They know if they are obvious about their self-absorbed traits, people won't like them. They believe they are "special" and entitled, but they know it would turn people off to let that be known. They know they must appear humble to be liked and revered. They know how to play people, how to charm them. They are master manipulators. They don't have empathy but have learned how to act empathetically. They will look you in the eyes, making you feel special and heard, make sounds and give looks that tell you they care, but they really don't. They mirror your emotions, so it seems like they have empathy. They have observed and learned how to appear to care. They thrive upon the attention of others. People who think or act as if they are amazing are their energy supply. They have people around them who adore them, respect them, revere them, see them as special and almost perfect, and in some cases seem to worship them.

The *Holy Hell* documentary provides a great example of a CN who led a cult with a large following who stayed with him for more than 20 years. The people who followed him aren't stupid. They are smart, kind, talented, tender people who were exploited, used, and convinced by a CN who appeared to love and care about them.

After living with a CN for a long time, cult deprogramming would actually be more beneficial than regular therapy with a therapist who does not understand this disorder. The effects of ending a relationship with a CN are similar to the effects of coming out of a cult. There is a lot of deprogramming that needs to happen in order to heal and see clearly. It is gut-wrenching in the first stages. If you watch the interviews at the end of *Holy Hell*, you will be amazed how much you will relate to what the people are thinking and feeling when they finally leave the cult leader. Even though you haven't come out of a cult, it is a profoundly similar experience.

Covert narcissists are likable to the outside world; they appear to be giving, humble, and kind. It is usually only the person who gets to know them intimately who sees the destructive traits. The rest of the world sees the façade, the "nice guy." Many therapists don't see through the mask and indeed are often impressed with how kind and aware the CN is. CNs seem to intensify their behavior around middle age; they rarely change because narcissists blame others and they usually don't think they have a problem.

Everyone loves CNs on a surface level. They tend to not have long-lasting friendships with people who know them deeply. They may have friends who have known them for years, but don't really *know* them. They are rarely without a partner. After they discard you, they usually move on quickly to another source—another target who will think they are so lucky to have found such a "nice guy" or "nice gal," just like you did in the beginning.

Many times daughters will consider their CN mom to be their best friend until later in life. It is a devastating realization when they recognize that the person who they thought loved them the most has actually been using them for years. They don't know what to believe anymore. This new awareness at the same time helps validate mixed messages they received growing up.

With CNs, it is all about them, but they know how to appear like it isn't. For example, they despise taking care of you when you are sick or recovering from surgery or an injury. They won't tell you that, but you feel it. They let you know through passive-aggressive ways. To family and friends, they will tell stories of how much they feel for you and appear to be taking exceptional care of you. They will come across as humble and will be sure to paint a picture of being a great caretaker. People around you will think how lucky you are to have someone so tender and loving by your side. The CN might even do things that look like they are taking care of you, but you will feel their resentment and will find yourself feeling alone and unsupported even though they are doing things that appear to be helpful.

An overt type might yell, call you names, and put you down by saying you're lazy and leave you to fend for yourself. You will feel like a covert thinks you are lazy, but they won't actually say it. You will feel how much they hate taking care of you, but they won't tell you that. They might word things in a way that gives you that message without directly putting you down. They will give you subtle messages that make you question yourself. You think you're just being too sensitive, reading into things, after all, they didn't actually tell you they think you're lazy. You will find yourself feeling badly for taking up their time, for inconveniencing them, and often end up apologizing for something. A CN will somehow manipulate things so the attention comes back to them, and you won't even notice it happening.

Covert narcissists will do things that are unkind to you, but somehow you will end up apologizing. It's not uncommon to feel like things are your fault. They aren't doing anything wrong, you convince yourself. When you are with a CN, you learn to ignore your gut feelings, your instincts, and over time believe the narcissist more than yourself. You will come to realize that the CN has slowly programmed you to see things the way they want you to see them, and gave you messages about yourself they want you to believe so they could keep controlling and manipulating you into continuing to be their "supply."

It is common for a survivor to have a hard time explaining what they have been through, because in their mind it doesn't sound that bad, and they fear people will think something is wrong with them. A phrase I hear often in local support groups is "crazy-making." Whenever one person uses that term, the room erupts in enthusiastic heads nodding, with smiles of empathy and relief that we are not the only ones who feel this way.

Many share how alone they feel, misunderstood by others who have not experienced this type of hidden abuse. A survivor will often start a sentence by saying, *"I know this might not seem that bad, and I'm embarrassed even saying it, but…"* After she is done sharing, the whole room is filled with other survivors saying, *"I totally get that!"*

When you first begin to realize a person you have loved and fully believed loved you is a covert narcissist, it is so hard to accept because you have seen them in such a different light for so long. It is a struggle for the brain to reconcile the man or woman you thought existed with the one who is now treating you with such anger and hostility. This is called cognitive dissonance—having two competing thoughts in your mind at the same time—and is part of the confusing feelings you might be experiencing. It is both painful and exhausting.

A covert narcissist can appear to be a loving partner for a long time. Their behavior often becomes more aggressive at the end of the relationship. This is when the narcissistic traits listed in the DSM-IV become more obvious; the sense of entitlement and superiority, the arrogant attitude, becomes more pronounced. They will still be covert with others, but the survivor will see and experience more of the overt traits coming to the surface. Their mask cracks when you, the survivor, begin trusting yourself. The stronger you become, the less they can control and manipulate you. When this happens, they no longer need you. You are no longer supplying them. This is when you feel their rage more than ever. This is when their behavior turns aggressive, cruel, and shocking.

After victims have left these relationships, they look back and realize how depressed they were for the majority of the relationship, how alone they felt, how they blamed their constant fatigue, health issues, and sadness on other things, not realizing the toll the relationship was taking on their body and spirit. As a result, it is common for victims to experience many health issues while they are in these toxic relationships. This is because covert narcissists slowly break your spirit over time without you seeing it, and you end up feeling like you were the problem. This emotional turmoil often manifests in various physical ailments.

I named this book *The Covert Passive-Aggressive Narcissist* because covert and passive-aggressive behaviors are both descriptive of a CN.

> *"They are both indirect ways to aggress, but they are most definitely not the same thing. Passive-aggression is, as the term implies, aggressing through passivity. In contrast, covert aggression is very active. When someone is being covertly aggressive, they are using calculating, underhanded means to get what they want or manipulate the response of others while keeping their aggressive intentions under cover"* (George Simon Jr., Ph.D., *In Sheep's Clothing: Understanding and Dealing With Manipulative People*).

It is a lot when you are first discovering things you haven't seen for years, putting together a picture that does not match what you thought was true. As you go through this book, take a deep breath (or many) to help your body as it is taking in new thoughts. We will dive deeper into what the behavior of a covert narcissist looks like and how this affects you; then we will talk about healing. That's where you get to exhale. Be extraordinarily kind to yourself throughout this discovery process. You deserve tenderness now more than ever.

A big part of healing is educating yourself.

Next, let's explore the common patterns of love bombing, devaluing, and discarding that are typical with covert narcissists.

2
The Three Phases:
Love Bombing, Devaluing,
and the Discard

There is a behavioral template that is typical of narcissistic abuse. It generally follows a pattern of three stages. The first stage is often referred to as love bombing (or the *idealization phase*), followed by devaluing, and finally the discard.

Describing these as stages can give the impression they manifest in sequential order. In some ways they do, and in other ways, the first two are experienced intermittently throughout the relationship until the discard. The cycle of all three can also repeat numerous times. The combination of the stages creates a dizzying whirlwind of emotion and confusion.

I will describe the stages in the context of a romantic relationship. But no matter what type of role this person has in your life, you will be able to recognize these three phases as they're explained and illustrated.

Love Bombing/Idealization Phase

Love bombing happens at the very beginning. This is where the groundwork is laid for you to fully trust and believe in this person for years to come. Because of your initial experience with them, you end up seeing everything they do through the lens of a good person, someone who cares about you, and someone you can trust with your heart.

This idealization phase usually lasts between six months and a year. This is generally the case, but not always.

Here are some descriptions people I interviewed gave me of the covert narcissists in their life during the love-bombing phase:

- *He was so kind.*
- *I felt so lucky to find her.*
- *He was different. He talked about his feelings.*
- *He asked me lots of questions about myself. He really wanted to know me. He seemed to really care.*
- *She was kind of shy.*
- *We were so much alike!*
- *He opened up to me about his abusive childhood. He was really honest and vulnerable.*
- *She was beautiful. Out of my league. I felt so lucky that she liked me.*
- *She was fun.*
- *He felt like my soul mate; like I had known him for a long time.*
- *He was interesting, intriguing.*
- *She was confident. She seemed to have her life together.*
- *He was great with kids.*
- *I felt lucky to be with her.*
- *He seemed tender.*
- *I felt safe with him.*

- *She was a really good listener.*
- *He was humble, kind, sensitive, and easy to connect with.*
- *He could get along with anyone. It was remarkable.*
- *She had everything I was looking for.*
- *He was spiritual, open, and philosophical.*
- *He was soft, which was so nice after experiencing a lot of anger in other relationships. I felt like I was going into this relationship with my eyes wide open.*
- *We talked about everything. The communication was great!*
- *I didn't know women like this existed!*
- *My friends and family were so happy for me that I had found such a great guy.*

Many told me they felt so at ease with the CN in the beginning stage.

> *"Although it feels amazing at first, this idealization is actually responsible for most of the damage when the relationship comes crashing down. They set a trap, and it's a trap no unsuspecting victim could hope to escape from"* (Jackson MacKenzie, *Psychopath Free*).

It is common for targets to say, *"We seemed so much alike."* This is because the covert narcissist mirrors you in the beginning, in a sense becomes you. They are observing you during this period. They will ride the wave of emotion you are feeling, so it feels like they are just as excited about this relationship as you are. This can carry on for a while. Many survivors look back and realize the excitement they felt, the energy of the relationship they so believed in, actually only came from them. They were the only source of life, but were under the illusion that it went both ways because the CN was mirroring their emotions.

CNs are often chameleons who can become whoever they are around. They don't have a strong sense of self. They pick up what a person wants, and they become that. Because of this, people are impressed with how well the CN can seem to relate to all types of people.

I spoke with one woman who would watch her narcissistic mom observe other people's insecurities and shower them with compliments and praise in those areas. The "targets" felt loved, seen, heard. Her mom didn't care about these people. She only wanted to look good and be impressive. She was using them for the attention and admiration she received from them. They were her energy supply.

Similarly, if a target is spiritually minded, it is common for them to feel like they have found their soul mate when they meet and date a CN. The connection feels like home. The CN mimics the same zeal for spirituality as the target genuinely has, which feels amazing to the victim. They are on the same page, it seems, but this is an illusion the CN creates.

It is common for CNs to test targets, to see if they are someone who will be a supply for a long time. Some of the women I talked to told me after six months to a year of dating, their CN started to have doubts about them. When the CN's negativity started, the target began to fight for the relationship because they believed in the connection so strongly. This made them perfect for the CN because they had proved they would stick with the CN through anything. This is the type of person a CN wants, the type of person they will groom.

When Sara dated Timothy, after a year of bliss there began to be issues in the relationship. They both agreed the relationship was worth fighting for, so they decided to go to therapy to figure things out. Sara thought it was amazing he was open to doing that. Most of the guys she had dated before would have never agreed to counseling. She believed it was one more impressive thing she had discovered about him.

What she didn't know was one of the worst things you can do is take a CN to therapy, especially in the beginning. Here is why: it's like a training ground for them. When the counselor tells them what they are doing wrong, how they are hurting you, it shows them which part of their mask is cracking. They learn what you want, and what they need to do to impress you as well as others. They do what the therapist suggests, impressing the target and the therapist. Their heart isn't in it, but they act like it is. The therapy sessions make you feel even more love and respect for them, once again sealing their image as the perfect mate, ensuring your love and loyalty for a very long time.

They learn your vulnerabilities and insecurities. CNs make sure to build you up and compliment you in these areas. It can feel like they are part of your healing. They will later use what they learn about you to trigger you, manipulate you, control you, and wound you—it becomes the biggest betrayal you have ever felt.

They also hook you with sympathy in the beginning. When Sara and Timothy were in therapy, he shared that he had never felt like anyone had really wanted to get to know everything about him. He expressed how much he longed to have someone take the time to pursue and love every part of him. This tugged at Sara's heartstrings. She is a caring woman, full of empathy. These are common traits of targets. She determined she would live her life doing just that. She would wholeheartedly get to know everything about him and love him like he had never experienced. She would give him all the attention he was craving, getting to know him in the way he longed to be known.

She did this for more than 25 years. When he would do things that weren't kind or respectful, she would see him as a wounded man who never got the love he needed and would excuse his behavior over and over because of it. He used her sympathy to control and manipulate her for decades. She would never have tolerated a lot of his behavior if it hadn't been for the groundwork laid in the love-bombing phase. Later, during the discard, Timothy told Sara it was clear to him that she never loved him.

After a survivor has experienced the discard phase and discovers they have been living with a CN for years, they feel embarrassed. *How did I not see this? How did I live with this for so long and be okay with it? What is wrong with me?*

It is important to know these are master manipulators who could fool just about anyone. People who haven't experienced this will never fully understand. When others hear the stories, they wonder why the survivor stayed for so long. It all begins with the love-bombing stage, which lays the foundation and sets everything in motion.

I want you to know that all the survivors I interviewed were intelligent people. Many of them were aware of psychological concepts. Some are in the mental healthcare field themselves. They are tender and have a tremendous amount of empathy. Many of them are also highly intuitive and aware of toxic behavior. They pick up when something is off with others. These are not naïve people. You can be super smart, as well as highly aware, and still be fooled by a CN.

Don't feel badly about yourself if you are a survivor. You've had enough of someone else making you feel badly about yourself. You are smart. You are strong. You got involved with someone who used your beautiful traits against you. That is not your fault. Millions of people are taken in by CNs. Be kind to yourself. All the kind words and actions from the CN during the love-bombing phase—all the attentiveness, the open communication, the compliments, the ease of it all—sets you up so that when the subtle devaluing begins, you don't even notice.

The Devaluing Phase

The word "devalue" says it all. At the beginning of a relationship with a covert narcissist, you feel incredibly valued. Then you begin to experience little things, statements they make, looks they give that begin to demean and devalue you. It is all very subtle. Over a long period of time, you are given the message by someone you love and trust that you have no value, no matter what you do, no matter how kind you are, no matter how much you do for them, you will never ever be enough for them. The cold, hard truth is you do not matter to them, and unfortunately, the message you end up receiving is that you do not matter, period.

The confusing thing is that while you are being devalued, you are also experiencing kindness. You receive beautiful love letters, affection, and loving gestures. You continue to believe this is a good relationship, and your partner loves you. You tell everyone around you how lucky you are to have the partner you do because you sincerely believe that. Your friends tell you they wish their husband/wife/partner was more like yours. However, though you are saying all of these things, you don't notice your self-image and self-worth slowly declining over time.

Through the years, you notice your health isn't great, you feel depressed, you aren't that happy, but you contribute these things to other things in life or blame yourself. The way your CN partner treats you goes unnoticed because it has become your normal. You don't notice the consistent devaluing because it is so subtle. You don't realize how you feel is a result of the trauma of living with an abuser.

Susan thought she had almost the perfect marriage. There were issues in their sex life she could never figure out, but everything else seemed great. They looked like the ideal couple to those around them. Like all victims, the discard phase was incredibly confusing for Susan, and excruciatingly painful. Her husband of 18 years was suddenly done with her, telling her how happy he was without her, blaming her for all kinds of things. He told her how unhappy he had been the whole time they were married and listed all the ways it was her fault. She was blindsided. *What in the world just happened?* She searched for answers to that very question.

As she learned about covert narcissism, Susan decided to read through her journals hoping she might see things that would help her make sense of it all. She wondered if she would see things in her writings that she didn't remember or hadn't noticed. *Had there been devaluing?* She didn't remember any. From her recollection, there hadn't been anything wrong with the marriage except for their sex life, which she had blamed herself for, anyway. But when she began reading from the time they met until the end of the relationship, she couldn't believe all she saw with more educated eyes. She was stunned when she read a part of her journal written while they were dating that said, *"I'm getting married soon, and I don't know why, but I have this strange fear that I will be taken advantage of and not even see it."* Her body knew from the very beginning. But like so many other times, she didn't trust it. She explained it away and for the next 18 years, she made countless excuses for his subtly demeaning behavior.

She also couldn't believe how many stories she came across in her journal showing how he had devalued her, sabotaging every vacation, birthday, and most holidays, times that meant something to her. All the stories started about a year after dating. A few months before they were married, she read about a trip he had gone on with a friend. She didn't hear from him for 10 days. Silence. No contact. No explanation. She had written in her journal how it felt like everything was on his time, what worked for him. She had also forgotten that she planned the entire honeymoon without his help, along with most of the wedding. He wouldn't show up for appointments when he had promised he would. Throughout the marriage, she saw how he did so many subtle acts to make her feel like she was too opinionated, too strong, too loud. He never acknowledged the mother she was, the wife she was, all she did for him and their family. He did not acknowledge any of her accomplishments. She never felt like she did enough to satisfy him. She was stunned as she read her own writings and found story after story about ways she was devalued for a long time.

It can be hard for people to understand why someone like Susan would stay with a man who would treat her that way. The love-bombing phase is incredibly powerful to the psyche. The devaluing stage is mixed with many loving acts. That's the incredibly confusing part.

At the same time he was devaluing Susan, he was also telling her how beautiful she was, giving her heartfelt cards. They were enjoying their time together, laughing about things, going on road trips, talking about their dreams, bonding over movies, books, and their mutual love of scuba diving. As the years passed, Susan found herself feeling worse about who she was. She was tired a lot, started experiencing allergies she had never had previously, she felt drained; like she didn't have the life inside her she used to have. She never associated these things with her marriage. She thought she just needed to figure out how to find more fulfilling work in her life. Maybe she needed to change how she eats, she thought, and exercise more. She had gained weight over the years. There were a lot of things to which she attributed the way she felt, but never to her husband.

As she read her journals, she also realized how alone she felt for the majority of the marriage. She would write about how lucky she was to have a husband like him. However, when she looked closer, she knew she didn't have a partner who really cared about her and who wanted the best for her.

This is such a difficult thing to grasp for victims of covert abuse. They convince themselves that the love they feel for their partner is also how their partner feels for them when in fact this is not true, and never was. Covert narcissists are not capable of real love. It was an illusion. That is an incredibly painful and disheartening realization.

The devaluing stage comes on subtly. They don't call when they said they would. They don't show up for appointments they'd agreed they would be at. Little acts that always come with excuses and send the target the message that they don't matter. The CN will do things like invite you to dinner, then when you arrive, it feels like they don't really want you there. You feel confused. They use the silent treatment to make you wonder if you are doing something wrong. A CN will control you through their moods, through looks they give you, through statements they make that may not seem like putdowns on the surface but make you feel badly about yourself. They will say nothing is wrong when it feels to you like something is wrong. During the devaluing phase, the victims are programmed to not trust themselves.

They will also devalue you by letting you think something is your fault when it is actually their issue. This is called projection. They project what is true about them onto you and you end up taking the blame without even noticing. The emotional needs of the victim are not of importance to the CN. Only the CN's desires, needs, or priorities matter to them.

It is also quite common for the victim to become responsible for everything. For instance, CNs don't like to help around the house. They will, but the target will feel their anger and irritation. After time, the victim learns it's just easier to do things on his or her own and to not ask for their help. The CN does not want to give in the relationship, only receive.

The mixed messages you get from a CN wreak havoc on your heart, mind, and body. They love bomb you and devalue you interchangeably for years. It is hard to make sense of it all because you have a solid belief that this person loves you and wants the best for you. The devaluing is often so subtle you don't notice yourself slowly declining as time goes by. Your self-worth and confidence are diminished, as well as your physical body. You feel more tired than normal. You slowly forget the free spirit you used to be and attribute things you are feeling to circumstances outside your relationship.

Targets receive lots of messages about themselves from the CN. Some things they say right to your face while other messages you receive from the CN's actions, looks they give, deafening silence, or the quiet rage emanating from them.

Real love never has mixed messages, and when the final discard happens, the truth about the CN that had been disguised for years come out.

The Discard

Most likely, the discard phase will feel like the most confusing and painful betrayal you've ever felt in your life. The person you have loved for years and who you believed loved you back is now saying the cruelest things—things you would have never imagined possible. They treat you like a child, "teach" you, punish you, and tell you how you should behave. They use every vulnerable thing you shared over the years to wound you in the most devastating way. They lash out at you with what feels like a firehose of insults. Sometimes they are calm and sound rational. Other times they rattle off a slew of words that make no sense, but deliver them as if they are completely normal. They also mix in words of love and affection. Then in the next breath, they tell you that you are vile and they are done with you. You have no idea who this person is. This is not at all who you thought you were living with all these years. You are left reeling.

The CN paints a false reality and says things about you that aren't true, but you question yourself, wondering if they are right because they sound so confident and act like they know more than you, and you feel like you can't think straight. They twist your words and confuse you with strange thinking. This leaves you questioning and doubting yourself constantly. You feel weak, confused, and fearful about your future. You feel alone.

This is the time when most survivors hear someone tell them their spouse/partner might be a narcissist. Sometimes this happens in therapy, in a meeting with a divorce attorney, during a search on the Internet when you are trying to figure out what is happening, or in talking to a friend. You find yourself spending all your free time watching YouTube videos, reading books and articles, seeking answers, and trying to make sense of this dizzying treatment you are experiencing.

Also, you might find yourself spying on your spouse/partner when you never considered doing this earlier in the relationship. You read their emails, check bank statements, wonder if they are having an affair. You ask them questions, and their answers don't make sense. In fact, they usually take your words and turn them against you to show you all the things that are "wrong" with you. They are defensive and angry. Then they are calm and devoid of feelings.

This is a bewildering time for so many reasons, one of which is the vast difference in how you feel versus how the CN feels. You are devastated. You are crying, curled up in the fetal position. They are done. They move out quickly. You are trying to find answers. They are not. You are deeply sad. They are letting you know they are the happiest they've ever been now that they aren't with you.

Many times they initiate the discard during a time that is special to you, or in a place that means a lot to you. They like to sabotage dates and places that are important to you. Bill told me his wife of 26 years told him she was done being married to him on his birthday. After years of telling him how handsome he was, how much she loved him, how amazing he was, she told him, *"I have never fully trusted you! Most women would have never lasted this long with you. I can't believe you haven't gotten therapy for your issues after all these years!"*

She kept going with a long list of other shocking and devastating statements. Similarly, when Karen's husband told her he wasn't sure if he wanted to be married to her anymore out of the blue after 17 years of being together, they were at her family's lake house where she had always felt the most safe and at peace growing up.

For many victims, the discard phase is the end of the relationship. Others experience a confusing cycle of breaking-ups and getting back together over years of dating a covert narcissist. I spoke with targets who had been in relationships like these for more than 10 years.

During the discard phase, you feel low about yourself. The CN paints a picture of you that is not accurate, but they make you feel like it is. There are enough grains of truth mixed in with bizarre distortions of reality that make you wonder if they are right about you. The CN also becomes more aggressive with their words and actions than you've seen before, but once again, you are the only one who sees this side of them. It is an incredibly conflicting time.

The discard phase is sudden and harsh. When they are done, they move on quickly and usually go right to another target. This is a stark contrast to how you feel. You are falling apart. You never expected this seemingly good marriage to end. While you are devastated at the thought of a relationship ending with someone you called your lover and best friend, the CN is not falling apart. They are bizarrely calm. You don't see them feeling sad. You feel their rage as it is directed at you, but they are not experiencing devastation and sadness, which makes you feel even crazier.

Sam and his CN partner, Adam, had been together for over 15 years. They were both spiritual thinkers. They had met at a yoga retreat and bonded over their similar thinking on life. After years of passivity, seeming so laid-back and easygoing, Adam became verbally abusive during the discard phase. There would be days when Sam would receive lists from his partner about everything that was wrong with him and would need to change for this relationship to work. Then the next day Adam would ask Sam if he wanted a foot massage, and would calmly tell him he was just flowing with the Universe, trusting the process. When Adam moved out of the house, he would lambaste Sam with abusive emails; then a few hours later would send an email thanking Sam for how well he had loved him over the years. A CN's behavior in this phase can be manic. You don't know what you are going to get from moment to moment.

This may happen while you are still living with your CN partner. *"I wish I could get rid of this anger and resentment I feel toward you,"* Don said to Emily with concern on his face, then seconds later in a fit of rage, he yelled at her for ruining every friendship he ever had in his life. Later, he brought home dinner for her and their kids and asked if she'd like him to make her favorite tea at bedtime. Blindsided, shell-shocked, and baffled are some other ways to describe this time when the CN cuts you off quickly and heartlessly.

The ironic thing is the CN usually initiates the end of the relationship, but it is often the survivor who actually files for divorce. The CN wants to be liked, to be seen as the victim, not the one who destroyed a family. They want people to feel sorry for them and see you as the one to blame. How they look to others is their top priority.

The CN will blame you for just about anything and everything. Emily counted more than 30 things Don had told her she would need to change about herself for the marriage to work. The thing you start noticing when you become aware of the issues with the

---

CN is that most of what they say about you is actually a projection of what is true of *them*.

After reading about this phase, you may identify that you are experiencing the discard phase right now. For many survivors, this is the time of avid research on the subject of narcissism. So many others are experiencing what you are at this moment. It's empowering and helpful to realize this. You are in the company of some amazing people just like you who also are looking for answers.

You may be feeling shocked, full of anxiety, alone, depressed. You may be having suicidal thoughts. Your body may feel like it's deteriorating. It's hard to focus at a time when you are making big decisions. You may be feeling reactive and impulsive. It's probably been a while since you were able to get a good night's sleep. This is all so common.

You have been through a lot and are still in the thick of it. You will get through this. You have come to the right place, and will someday see things clearly. Breathe. Reach out to friends and family who love you. Keep learning. Join a support group. Meetup dot com is a good place to look for these. Give yourself permission to fall apart, sometimes. Hire a good attorney who knows about narcissism if this is a divorce situation. Above all, know that you deserve kindness and respect.

I will talk more in-depth about what it is like to divorce a CN in chapter nine and also more about their traits and ways they manipulate and control throughout the book. Before I do that, I want to talk about you—the target, the victim, and the survivor.

Let's look at beautiful and valuable you.

3

Traits of Targets

Covert narcissists will seek out a certain type of person for intimacy. They know what traits someone needs to have to be able to control and manipulate them. For instance, they wouldn't be able to use their emotions and comments to manipulate if the person didn't have empathy, compassion, and a nurturing heart. They wouldn't be able to convince someone to take the blame for something that isn't their fault if the person was not self-reflective.

As I interviewed survivors and listened to victims of narcissistic abuse in local support groups, I found it fascinating to see so many traits in common. Here is what I found. These people are smart. They are responsible. They are the ones who hold things together; often they are the heart of the family. They do almost everything in the home and as parents. These are people on which you can rely. They are loyal, faithful, and resilient women and men.

Survivors often are the dreamers, the optimists of the world, seeing the best in others. They are loving, kind, and pure-hearted. They trust the word of others because *they* are trustworthy. It is not in them to lie and so it is difficult for them to believe someone they love would lie to them. Lying, controlling, and manipulating go against how they are intrinsically made. They were made to love and be loved; that is when they thrive.

Targets are honest and real. They do not pose. They do not pretend to be someone they are not. What you see is what you get with them, and that is incredibly refreshing. As survivors, they tend to be flexible and easygoing. Planning an event with them is a delight. They are easy working partners and generous with their time.

I was recently at a support group where we considered branching to create a women's-only group. A few of us were discussing what we needed to do to make the change. We talked about how we would get the money to pay for the dues and who would coordinate certain aspects, essentially all the details of what needed to be done to make this transition. It was the easiest conversation in the world. One lady offered to pay for all of it. Others said they'd be happy to split the cost. No one was stressed. No one was in a hurry. No one was out for themselves. Everyone was generous, not wanting the action steps to fall on one person's shoulders. It was peaceful, loving, productive, and easy.

Meeting survivors has been like finding gold in this world. These are people who are not interested in drama. They love peace and harmony. They are self-reflective women and men who are interested in growing and bettering themselves. They look to see where they can improve. They don't blame others; they take responsibility for their own behavior. If they are feeling hurt or frustrated in a relationship, they often say, *"I'm feeling this..."* or *"When you said that, I felt this..."*

They won't tell you what they think is wrong with you. This great quality, however, is used against them by a CN. CNs will blame them for things, and because survivors are people who look at themselves, they will be open to seeing if they are to blame. Often, the victim finds himself or herself thinking, *There must be some truth to it. This person knows me. They live with me, so there might be something I need to change here.* It's difficult for targets to recognize how badly they are being treated and they often accept way more responsibility than is necessary or true.

CNs are skilled at phrasing things so you don't notice their cruel behavior. Emily's counselor told her, *"Your husband has this amazing ability to start out a conversation appearing so humble and kind. You become so impressed you don't notice how he blames you by the end. You take that on and feel shame. You end up apologizing for something that isn't even your fault, but he sets you up to feel like it is."*

Targets are trusting people. They are nurturing, forgiving, and compassionate. They are full of empathy, and this, sadly, is one of the most exploited traits by a CN. Your empathy is a big reason they chose you. They prey on this treasured part of you with displays of emotion, manipulative comments, and actions intended to control and punish you.

One woman with whom I talked said her brother had passed away recently. She was very close to him. On the anniversary of his death, her husband suddenly sunk into a deep depression. Because he did this, she didn't feel she was allowed to be sad. She turned her attention onto him to make sure he was okay. CNs do subtle things like this to control you, to keep the attention on them, and to sabotage times that are sacred to you.

Another example of how a CN will shift the focus back on them is demonstrated by Wendy's dramatic story. Wendy's eyes had been opened to something she experienced years ago, when her husband exploited her sensitive heart. Her care and concern for him brought her to a place of feeling bad; she ended up taking care of him after he had been cruel and dishonoring to her. Her husband was on the phone with his mom. When they were done talking, he told Wendy that his mom had said Wendy was controlling and manipulative. They had been married for about 10 years at the time. Here and there her husband would go through times of questioning Wendy, telling her things his family would say about her to see what she thought. This time after starting to defend herself, Wendy stopped and said,

> *"You know what, I have been defending myself to you for 10 years. If you don't know who I am by now, I don't know what to tell you. You're just going to have to decide for yourself what you think is true about me."*

Wendy's husband responded with silence, left the room, and went out to their back yard to think. After a few minutes he returned and suddenly fell to the ground in agonizing pain. He said his back hurt and he couldn't get up. He stayed on the floor all night. Wendy felt horrible. She brought him containers to urinate in when he needed them throughout the evening. She felt like she was the cause of all the stress he felt. If she didn't exist, he wouldn't be feeling this. There would be no issues between him and his mom. In the morning he asked her to call the ambulance because he was still in great pain. They wheeled him out, gave him some shots, and he came home pain-free. The pain never came back. Quite a quick recovery for such excruciating chronic pain over a two-day period...

This is dramatic, but not unusual for a CN. Many survivors have told me stories of CNs faking injuries and illnesses, some for years. They will go to great lengths to make you feel bad and turn the attention back on them. Wendy's husband was cruel to tell her what his mom said. As long as you are feeling bad, shame, they have you. You are under their control. He should have defended Wendy to his mom. He should have never told her about the phone conversation, knowing it would only hurt her. That is what love looks like. The real thing, not the illusion you get used to with a CN. This tactic works on targets because they are tenderhearted, sensitive, caring, and trusting people.

I will say again about targets I interviewed and observed: they are *smart* individuals. They have been manipulated to think they are not, but these people *are* intelligent. Most of them could have their master's in psychology after all their research and experience. Many of them are now helping others who are going through their own pain. These are beautiful souls. They love solutions where everyone wins. They are team players who will have your back and be your biggest fan. I have experienced such love and encouragement from each and every one of the targets I've met. I feel grateful to know them. They are wonderful listeners, independent, hard-working individuals, although most of them have been told they are lazy by their CN, which is a common putdown and the furthest thing from the truth.

During more than one interview, I found myself sitting across from a man or woman, watching their body physically shake as they shared their story. My own tears would come. I have a tender heart, and a fierce one, like many survivors. These people are the cream of the crop. They are the ones we are so fortunate to have on this planet. They bring life and love wherever they go. For me to see each of these treasured beings have their spirits crushed, their souls wearied, and their hearts wounded over and over, year after year—it did something to me. I felt angry. Really angry. This was wrong. The beautiful person in front of me had been leveled, bewildered, and emotionally assaulted for years. Their pain was palpable.

The more I heard, the more motivated I became to write this book. These survivors did not deserve any of this. One person—in some cases multiple CNs—caused their bright light to almost go out, and that is not okay.

Targets are strong people. They are mightier than the CN in their life could ever imagine. Every survivor has the capacity to open their eyes and see the truth of what they have been through, then become a force to be reckoned with. They will be a force for good, of course, because that is who they are.

That is who you are.

Now it's time to educate you, dear powerful one, on the traits and manipulative tactics of a covert narcissist, so you can finally see clearly and make your way home.

4

Traits of a Covert Narcissist

The DSM-IV gives us a list of core traits of narcissists. However, there are other traits I have found to be common in covert narcissists.

Before I list them, it is important to note that there is a spectrum with narcissists. On a scale from one to ten, you may have a CN in your life who is lower on the spectrum. They may exhibit a few of these traits. It's also possible that you may know a CN who fits almost all, if not all of them. Narcissists can also be a combination of covert and overt.

They Do Not Have a Strong Sense of Self

Covert narcissists don't have a solid identity, a knowing of who they are. If you think of certain people in your life who you know well, you would probably have a lot to say to describe them. They are distinguishable. With CNs, the description seems more generic. *"They are really nice,"* or *"They are easy to get along with,"* are common descriptions, but it rarely goes further than that. There is a feeling of, *"Who are they really?"* If you look at CNs, you will notice a hollow feeling about them, almost vacant. They can feel like a shell of a person.

CNs often are chameleons, becoming the people they are around.

It's common for a survivor to talk about the beginning stages of their relationship and say how amazingly similar they and their spouse/partner were. Then, after the discard when the CN begins dating someone else, they begin to become just like their new target.

Silent Rage

CNs have a lot of rage inside them. They may not yell, or get violent, but you can feel their quiet rage. They mask it around others, but when you live with them, it can feel like being next to a dormant volcano that could erupt at any moment. Their rage controls the climate of the home and keeps people feeling like they are walking on eggshells. This is one way they maintain control of people close to them.

This type of action immediately resonated for Mary. Over the years, she would ask her husband, *"Are you okay? You seem angry."* He would respond by saying calmly, *"No. Just tired."* Then he would stay quiet while Mary wondered who to trust: her own instincts or his word. Her body could feel his anger, but why would he lie? She chose to trust him and ignore her own feelings. This is a component of gaslighting (which I will discuss further in the next chapter) and other manipulative tools used to get the victim to slowly, over time, believe the CN over their own inner guidance.

Many victims told me they felt responsible for their CN spouse's or parent's anger. They get the unspoken (and sometimes spoken) message they are the cause of the CN's rage. This could not be further from the truth, but it is what the CN wants the victim to believe.

Lying

CNs are incredibly good at hiding and masking their lies. Many victims find it hard to believe they ever heard lies from their CN. CNs rarely seem like people who would lie. They come across as dependable and trustworthy. Targets in relationships with CNs often feel they have open communication about everything. However, toward the end of the relationship, they start noticing things that make them wonder.

During the discard phase, it's not uncommon for the targets to find themselves spying on their partners, which is something they would have never dreamed of doing before investigating this behavior. Reading texts and emails late at night, they begin to uncover things their CN has not shared, and sometimes catch them in outright lies.

If a target brings any of this to the CN's attention, the CN will find a way to turn it around and make something the target's fault. Because trust has been built over time, even the most bizarre excuse from the CN makes the victim still consider their explanation. It's so hard for them to imagine their partner would lie after years of seeing them as trustworthy.

Toward the end of her marriage, Valerie started feeling strange about a friendship her husband, Jack, was having with a guy he had just met. She was happy for him, but at the same time it seemed and felt odd. For instance, they would go on late-night walks together. Sometimes he wouldn't return home until three o'clock in the morning. They would send each other pictures of themselves. Jack would get giddy every time he got to see his new friend. There were days he would ask Valerie if she could leave the house so he could have some quiet time to himself. She would and later found out he used that time to have lunch with his friend.

During this time, Jack was pulling more and more away from Valerie and their kids. She was concerned and mentioned it to him. She got the courage during one conversation to ask if he had romantic feelings for his new friend. She told him it was okay if he did; in fact, it would help make sense of things in their marriage. The dormant volcano exploded. Jack hurled accusations at her, saying she had ruined every male friendship he had ever had and now she was ruining this one.

Weeks went by, then Valerie came across an email from the friend to her husband that said, *"When are you coming over? My dick isn't going to suck itself."* She showed Jack the email. He brushed it off, saying, *"Oh, that was just us messing with you because we were angry at what you were insinuating."*

To the outside world, it was obvious what was occurring, but Valerie had been with Jack for a long time and had never known him to lie. She accepted his explanation. She had gotten so used to accepting things being her fault that she didn't recognize what was right in front of her or acknowledge that even if he was telling the truth, it was an incredibly cruel, immature, and disrespectful act. He also never once addressed her feelings. They did not matter to him. She didn't notice this because she had lived with subtle messages that she did not matter and was not worthy of respect for a very long time.

When a CN lies and you confront them about it, they will not acknowledge your feelings as would happen in a healthy relationship. They will never put themselves in your shoes. Instead, they will deflect, so the negative attention gets turned around on you and off of them. They will blame you for their bad behavior: *"You made me do it, you drove me to it, this is your fault…"*

Hoovering

Hoovering is a technique used by some CNs to make it hard for victims to move on. It is how they pull their targets back into their sphere of influence.

I spoke with several men and women who were in relationships that had long cycles of breaking up and getting back together. This was the case with Rose. As soon as she would pull back from the relationship, the CN would pursue her more. He would apologize, explain away his hurtful behavior in terms that made sense to her and even triggered her compassionate heart. He would be loving and tender, saying everything she longed to hear. He was romantic and thoughtful. In her mind, she felt like she was seeing the real man return, the one with whom she fell in love and believed with all her heart. She felt loved and relieved; she took him back. Things were great for a while—until the cycle began again. He would become distant, pulling away, acting in ways that confused her, doing passive-aggressive things that devalued her; then she would pull away, rethink things, and he would come back as a prince charming again…

CNs observe you and groom you, and they know exactly what you need to hear to get you back. For them, it's all about control.

Constant Criticism

CNs will constantly criticize and judge you. Because they are covert, they do it in ways that are not always obvious. This enables them to control you as your self-worth slowly declines. Over time, this works on your sense of value. You end up seeing yourself as being not loveable, not wanted, and either too much or not enough.

The CN will judge you and put you down for the strangest things. Emma said her mom would often make underhanded comments to her siblings about how Emma doesn't like to stand for long periods of time. In another example, Marcy's ex-spouse would give her "constructive criticism" because he was "concerned" about the way she dressed and presented herself.

The constant criticism chips away at your sense of who you are, resulting in you believing the CN is superior and knows more than you, creating an unhealthy dependence on him or her. This weakens you over time and makes you vulnerable to their manipulation tactics.

The CN's criticism increases and becomes more blatant when you begin to stand up for yourself.

Jealousy

Sam's CN partner never said he was jealous of him, but Sam would feel like things were different when he started experiencing more success and happiness in his life. He started noticing that his partner wouldn't have big reactions when Sam would tell him exciting things that were happening in his life. His partner would become more withdrawn and disengage from him.

Sally's mom would sabotage times Sally had with her friends. Sally was so excited to meet a group of girls after they moved to a new town. One night, she had a sleepover, and her mom made it awkward and uncomfortable. Then her mom would ground Sally for unreasonable things to keep her away from her new friends.

Many survivors have a hard time explaining how their CN was jealous of them. It's more a feeling they gathered when they lived with them. Narcissists are deeply unhappy people. They get jealous of you when you are experiencing life and happiness. They do not want you to be happy and strong, as those feelings threaten their ability to control you.

They Project Their Own Issues Onto You

If you think about all the things the CN in your life has told you are wrong with you, my hunch is if you really look at the list, most of the statements are actually true of *them*. CNs don't acknowledge their own issues. Instead, they project them onto you. This means you end up feeling guilt and shame for things that are not even your issues.

Amy put some of her and her husband's joint savings into a real-estate business venture. She spent a lot of time and effort on this project for over a year. At first, things were going well for her, then the market crashed. She lost the money she had used to fund the project and had to take more money out of their account to cover the loss. She was devastated. This was the first time she had done anything like that. It took courage, research, and many hours of labor on her part. The work she did was amazing, but in her eyes she had failed her family. She cried on and off for weeks feeling so guilty she had done this. Her husband didn't yell at her, didn't say hurtful things; instead, he said nothing. He was punishing her through silence. Without saying a word, he was speaking volumes. She never took a risk like that again.

A healthy, loving, empathetic spouse would have said something like,

> *"So it didn't work out this time. You did an amazing job. I'm so impressed with what you were able to accomplish! You've learned a lot. You know what to do and not do now, so go out there and find another investment. I know this one will be a success. You'll do great."*

This response would have changed everything for her—to be seen, believed in, and respected. Instead she sobbed, felt so much guilt, and experienced shame. The message from her CN was that she made terrible decisions, wasn't good with money, and should never think about doing anything like that again.

Later, she was able to see that the truth was her husband was the one who was not good with money and had made terrible decisions, losing money himself. He was projecting his own issue with money onto her. He had manipulated her for years, leading her to believe she was terrible with money, so she didn't notice this was actually his issue, not hers. The way he went about giving her this message was so covert she took the shame and blame for years without seeing the truth.

Toward the end of these relationships, the CN will be more direct about what they think of you. Here are some common things I have heard survivors say they have been told by their CN: *You are controlling, manipulative, inconsiderate; you don't care about my feelings; you are lazy; it's all about you; I can't trust you; you only did that so you would look good to others.* Notice a pattern here? These are all traits of narcissists. They don't take responsibility for their own behavior. Instead, they project what is true about them onto you.

Another way they do this is by sharing their "fears" with you. *"I'm afraid you are going to cheat on me."* Later, you find out they had an affair. *"I have this fear that you are manipulating me."* They are the one manipulating you. CNs will manipulate you by putting the focus on you. They seem completely sincere, so you don't notice these are actually their problems.

They will say things like, *"I am taking responsibility for my part of this, but you aren't taking any."* This makes you wonder if it is true. You question yourself. *Maybe I'm not. Am I?* They throw curveballs at you all the time in order to deflect the truth that they are lying. They do it in a way that gets you spinning and self-doubting, so you don't notice the lie. They are kings and queens of saying things that aren't true, but they say them with such surety and confidence, it's hard to doubt them. No wonder you end up doubting yourself with all the smoke and mirrors to keep you confused and under their control.

There is something else that happens, especially if you are empathic in a relationship with a CN. You find yourself feeling things that you later notice are gone after you don't live with them anymore.

Megan had a lot of self-hatred while she was married to a CN. She would take pictures of her body as a reminder of how much she hated the way she looked. Megan would look at the pictures and feel disgust as well as anger at herself for gaining weight over the years. This was a way of punishing herself. After 15 years of marriage, the CN left. Soon after he did, she noticed her self-hatred was gone. She is the type of person who easily picks up on what others are feeling and wondered if she had actually been feeling

53

the CN's self-hatred, which had nothing to do with her. He never let on how much he hated himself, but subconsciously projected his issue onto her. He knew about the pictures, but never took the time to hold her, to tell her how beautiful she was. He never felt sorrow for her pain, never felt empathy. He allowed her to believe the lies of self-hatred.

Their Words Don't Match Their Actions

When Bonnie was in mediation trying to agree on a parenting plan with her CN husband Charles, he kept telling his attorney and the mediator how much he wanted the best for his kids, how much he cared about them, and how concerned he was with the way Bonnie parented them. His attorney would tell the mediator compassionately, *"He's just trying to do the right thing."* Then he asked for the least amount of time commitment possible to see his kids. Bonnie told me he sees his kids for an average of one meal a week and continues to tell her how terrible a parent she is. A CN's hypocrisy can last for years after the marriage has ended. Soon after our conversation, Bonnie called me to tell me she had just received an email from her ex-husband after being divorced for five years. Though he continued to only see their kids for one meal a week, the message said he and his girlfriend were working really hard to undo the terrible job Bonnie is doing as a parent.

CNs are such convincing people that it is easy to only listen to their words and not notice their actions or lack thereof. This is especially true in the area of intimacy, where they know they have a tremendous amount of power to manipulate.

When Ann was married to Tim, their sex life was confusing, which is common in relationships with CNs. She had absolutely no sex drive or desire to be with him and couldn't figure out why (her body knew she wasn't safe with him). She felt terrible that she was depriving him and he, of course, would let her know often how hard this was for him. Thinking something was wrong with her, she tried therapy, hormones, dietary changes, and read sex books over the years they were together. Nothing changed. She felt so much guilt and shame. Her husband was passive about it, waiting for her to fix herself. At the end of the marriage, he yelled at her, saying she had never tried and how much he had. This wasn't true, but she felt even more shame hearing his words, somehow believing that he had tried when in fact he had done nothing, putting it all on her. He had spent their years together letting her take the blame, not admitting his own sexual issues, not caring about her feelings, and not helping in any way. His inaction went unnoticed, and his words damaged what she thought was true about herself. It turned out the problems were actually about him because he had unresolved sexual issues he projected onto her. A CN's words are designed to distract you so you don't notice how their actions don't match.

They Are Emotionally Disconnected

It is difficult to have a real connection with a CN. This can be a trait that is hard to put into words because it's something you feel inside you when you are around someone, but have a difficult time explaining. Something feels off about them, but you can't put your finger on it.

There is almost a robotic feeling about CNs, as if they are scripted. They are so used to being chameleons, posing as someone they are not, it's like their real self is unattainable. Healthy people feel and express their thoughts and emotions in a genuine way.

CNs tell you what they think you want to hear in order to achieve their agenda.

You think a CN is connecting with you when both of you are talking about feelings, but when you look at your history, you were the one carrying the connection. Because they don't have a strong sense of self, CNs are not able to connect with anyone on a deep level. They will have times of opening up, sharing what they are feeling, but it feels different than when you talk to someone who is connected with who they are, someone who is genuine and real with no agenda.

CNs will cry or rage in ways that seem over the top. Annie's partner would get irate when his sports team would lose on TV. His mood would be affected for the next few days. But when Annie almost lost her life, he seemed indifferent, annoyed that he had to take care of her during her recovery from a car accident. It's like the CN's emotions are displaced because they are so disconnected with who they are. This characteristic makes them dangerous individuals because they have the capacity to hurt you and others without feeling remorse.

The fundamental part of human connection is to be able to feel with each other. Without that, there is no possibility of a relationship with real depth and authentic love. It is baffling, as CNs act like they care, but actually don't. Because they are emotionally disconnected, they are unable to experience deep intimacy and will always leave you feeling void of real connection.

Flying Monkeys

"Flying monkeys" are people in the narcissist's life who act on their behalf. These are the CN's biggest fans. They have a solid belief the narcissist is the victim, and that *you* are to blame for a multitude of things.

These people add to the already overwhelming hurt caused by a CN. They will do things like smear your name to others, send you scathing emails telling you how you are to blame for everything, testify against you in court, and sabotage you in any way they can. A CN brings you to a place where you doubt yourself; the flying monkeys add to this because they are also telling you things that are "wrong" with you. This compounds the self-doubt, confusion, and crazy-making behavior you already experience from the narcissist.

Flying monkeys are the narcissist's enablers, their loyal team of supporters. Many times, these people do not know what they are doing. They believe wholeheartedly in the CN just like you did for years. They are being fed convincing lies just like you were. CNs are master manipulators, and their flying monkeys are often additional victims of their deception.

They Take Credit for Your Ideas

Samantha didn't think much of it at first when she would whisper a funny comment into her husband's ear, and he would immediately repeat what she said to people around them and soak in the laughter and attention. Samantha enjoyed providing him with an experience that felt good to him. She enjoyed that he thought her comment was funny enough to share. But after year after year of him doing this and never giving Samantha the credit, it began to seem odd to her.

This is also a common trait seen in the workplace between coworkers. It adds to a CN's main goal of putting as much attention and accolades on themselves while giving the target the message they are unimportant, only there for the CN, and not worthy of praise or attention.

They Withhold Praise and Recognition

When Annie was researching and learning more about covert narcissism, she found herself recalling events in her marriage that she had forgotten and now saw them in a different light. One day while clearing out her garage, she came across a painting she had created years before. She looked at it and realized her husband had never said a word about it. Her friends and family had raved, saying she should do an art show. They were amazed at her talent. Annie began to reflect on all of her accomplishments over the 19-year marriage and realized that not once had her husband said, *"Wow. That's amazing! I'm so impressed!"*

On the other hand, she recalled all the times she had given him praise, complimented him, and told him how impressed she was at things he had done. She had always supported and encouraged him.

When you study narcissism, you start noticing abuse behavior you had missed. What often goes unnoticed is what wasn't there.

It was an eye-opening realization to Jen that not one time in 25 years did her CN husband ever acknowledge the great job she had done as a mom to their children, all the times she had volunteered to help people in need, and the way she had always taken care of things to ease his load. Instead, she felt like no matter what she did, it was never enough.

After interviewing people who have experienced the targeting of covert narcissism, I decided to also talk to women and men who are married to healthy, normal spouses. When you are used to the illusion of love, it is helpful as you are healing to see what the real thing looks like. It was always the same story I heard from them—so much praise. Liz has been married for 25 years to her husband and says anytime she accomplishes something or helps him out in any way, he praises her, thanks her, and appreciates her. He lets her know often how grateful he is for her. This does not happen in a relationship with a covert narcissist. You get the message you don't matter.

Connie moved every couple years during her 15-year marriage to Dave because of his job as a sports coach. She had been a stay-at-home mom taking care of their three kids through all the moves. She had been flexible and adapted to change well, making the best of things. Dave was gone a lot during their years together, so she took care of things at home while he was away so he was able to move up in his career without worrying about things at home. He never once told her how much he appreciated all she did, or otherwise recognize that she could have pursued her own career. After their divorce, he told her he never needed her. She had nothing to do with helping him get where he was in his career, and he could have just hired a nanny. That is another cruel and heartless message from the narcissist: *you are easily replaceable.*

CNs are not interested in building you up as a person, in seeing you happy, or in cherishing you for all that you do. A relationship with a CN must be all about them. When it stops being that way, they have no more use for you and move on to their next target.

They Sabotage Birthdays, Holidays, Vacations, and Meaningful Dates

Whenever I ask survivors what their birthdays and holidays were like with their CN, the answer is always the same. Across the board, whether the abuser was a parent or a romantic partner, they describe these special dates as being terrible.

> *"I can't even tell you what was wrong each birthday. I just remember calling my best friend almost every year crying. I never felt like I had a reason to cry. He always did something, gave me a gift, but it felt like he dreaded that day and never enjoyed celebrating me. I would usually end up apologizing for something. It felt like something was always my fault."*

> *"My mom always made a big deal of my birthday, but I hated that day. It was all about her. The parties were lavish. Everyone was always so impressed by them, but I would hear my mom complaining about how much work she had put into it. She would talk about the homemade cake she made and how expensive everything was and how hard I was to shop for. It was exhausting, and I felt like I was the cause of her stress. I would try to help, but it was never enough."*

> *"Christmas always felt like a struggle. He became depressed every year. I felt bad because he would tell me how he missed the magic of his childhood Christmases and he felt sad every year that he didn't feel that same feeling. I would try to make it beautiful and magical and special, but his mood never changed. Then he would say things to me that gave me the message I was doing things wrong. It was exhausting."*

CNs are very passive. They put the responsibility on you to make sure they are happy and blame you when they're not.

"He was a nightmare on every vacation. I did everything, planned everything, tried to make it enjoyable for all of us, but no matter what, he would be moody, irritable, and grumpy the whole time. He would sulk and complain about the littlest things. We would be in the most beautiful places, and he would find something that would make him angry. I somehow felt like it was my fault, feeling responsible for his unhappiness."

Narcissists do not like to celebrate you. They do not like it when you are happy. They want the attention on them, so they sabotage days and events that are special to you like Mother's Day, Father's Day, holidays, birthdays, even anniversaries of people you were close to you that have passed away. They do this through their moods, by complaining, making you feel badly about something, anything. They make it about them in all kinds of ways.

There are so many examples of this dampening effect. In one example, Jeanine loved to travel. It was the one thing in her life that gave her the most joy. She came to life every time she was able to explore new places, visit friends, and have new experiences. One day, her husband sat her down and broke the news to her. He told her he had just talked to a psychic about her and the psychic said she was traveling too much.

CNs will go to bizarre measures to sabotage you and keep you from enjoying your life. When you start doing things you want to do—things that delight you—they lose control of you and don't have the power to keep you down. They use whatever means they have to punish you and keep you contained.

They Belittle You and
"Teach You Lessons"

CNs will belittle you in ways that are indirect and sometimes not noticeable. There is an overall message from them that they know more than you and you are not doing it right. This gets more aggressive during the discard phase.

This can look like advice they give you or "constructive criticism." This can be especially cloaked when they are parents. They come across like they are just trying to help guide you, but you leave feeling disempowered and scared of life, believing you don't have what it takes to figure things out. You get the subtle message you are doing things wrong, but it comes in the form of "concern for you." You feel the life go out of you and don't know why.

During the discard phase, Jeanine's husband moved out of the house, closed their bank accounts without telling her, and met her to discuss how money was going to work from that point forward. She was a stay-at-home mom taking care of three kids, completely dependent on his income. He told her how much he would send her each month. She told him that was less than half of what she usually needs for herself and the kids. He told her the same psychic who had previously said she traveled too much also told him that Jeanine had come to this planet to learn how to work hard and not to expect others to support her. He was "helping her" learn her lesson by keeping the money from her.

Similarly, Mary remembers times her CN would become extra nice to people when she was being direct and bold with them. He was letting her know indirectly that her behavior was too much as he tried to counteract her strength. He would also gently put his hand on her back to steer her away from them, to stop her from talking. This furthered the message that it was not okay for her to stand up to people. He was more concerned about what the other people thought than about standing by and supporting her. He was "teaching" her how to behave.

The way CNs belittle spouses who have stuck by them for years, been faithful to them, and loved them is appalling, disturbing, and inhumane. Survivors often feel like prisoners in their own homes during the later stages of the relationship. They are told what they should and should not be doing and treated like children who need guidance. It is so upsetting to see these goodhearted people breaking down as they tell me story after story of demeaning treatment they have received by someone who they thought loved them.

They Are Self-focused and Emotionally Immature

It's been remarkable to hear so many stories of the self-centered and emotionally immature behaviors of CN parents. Here are three examples that may resonate with your own experiences.

Bill's wife had issues with alcohol abuse. She had sought treatment for it and learned different tools to help herself. She would get frustrated with her teenage kids when they didn't understand her process and wanted them to be more enthusiastic about her healing. *"They need to understand what I'm going through!"* she would tell Bill. She favored one child because she listened to her problems and alienated the others, who didn't want to hear.

Catherine's husband loved the movie Phenomenon. He was upset at his teenage daughter because he kept trying to get her to watch it with him and she kept turning him down. He wanted her to get into his world, to see what he was passionate about. She never felt like watching the movie with him. He asked Catherine to talk to their daughter about this for him.

Jen's husband barely spent time with their kids after the divorce. Their son kept trying to get together with him, but each time his dad turned him down with some excuse. One day, their son won free tickets to a movie. He was so excited and asked his dad if he could take him. Jen's ex told him he couldn't because he was going to see the Dodgers play with Sara (his new target). Their son told his dad he was frustrated and disappointed that he didn't see him very much. Exasperated, his dad told their son,

> *"Look, you have to understand I have a lot of people I need to take care of. I'm an uncle, a boyfriend, a brother, a son, and I have things to do. And aren't you excited for me that I get to see the Dodgers?!"*

With CNs, everything truly is about them.

There Are Always Strings Attached

When CNs do something nice for you, it doesn't feel like unconditional love, like they just enjoy treating you because it makes you happy. It feels like there are strings attached and you will need to pay them back later in some way.

The same is true of gifts they give you. It never feels like they had so much fun shopping for you and feel so much delight in giving you gifts. It feels like it was a drudgery to them, and you better know how much trouble it caused them, and you better feel bad, and you better give back to them in whatever ways they demand later—and you better take care of their feelings after they went to so much trouble.

This applies to times they show loving acts to you, like holding the door open, rubbing your feet, listening to you, doing nice things. It all feels like it will come back to bite you and be used against you in some way if you don't cater to them. It doesn't feel like clean love. It doesn't feel like it comes from someone who cherishes you and enjoys loving you.

In a normal relationship, there is a natural back and forth that happens. With CNs, the rules are different. It is all about them in every area. This is a one-way relationship.

They Use People

CNs use people to get what they want. You can feel it when they act like they are listening to someone. It doesn't feel genuine. They don't seem fully engaged—like they are really there with the person. Sometimes they talk to people to gain information from them, sometimes to get sympathy, other times to help them get where they want to be in their career. Another motivation is to get people on their side as is the case with their flying monkeys.

I also spoke to one target who woke up to the fact that her boyfriend was a CN by watching a scene in a movie. Film can be a helpful medium. If you want to see covert narcissism in action, watch the television series *House of Cards*. At the end of the episode "Chapter Three," Frank Underwood (played by Kevin Spacey) is manipulating a couple who have just lost their child. He comes across like he cares about them tremendously, but in fact, he is just trying to further his political agenda. Toward the end of his conversation with them where he is trying to gain their trust, he looks at the camera to reveal what he is really thinking and says, *"What you have to understand about my people is that they are a noble people. Humility is their form of pride. It is their strength. It is their weakness. And if you can humble yourself before them, they will do anything you ask..."* He didn't care about their hearts, their grief. He was out for himself, and he was using innocent people to get there. That is what CNs do. Their motives are not pure. Their lack of empathy results in a lack of conscience. People are in their lives to be used, not loved.

They Are Dizzying Conversationalists

Once their mask has begun to crack and their deplorable behavior becomes more pronounced, conversations with CNs leave you feeling muddled and exhausted. You find yourself questioning reality and your own sanity.

CNs throw a conglomeration of words your way that makes you feel jumbled and shaken. You feel like your forehead is in a perpetually confused wrinkle. You feel like screaming as you wonder what in the world is happening. At the same time, CNs appear as normal human beings who are making complete sense.

Before you realize a CN is a narcissist, you see them as a normal person with empathy, someone who doesn't manipulate. You trust their words are coming from a place of love. You give them the benefit of the doubt, and essentially project your own good qualities onto them. So when they hurl statements at you that wound, bemuse, and sound right as well and totally wrong at the same time, it is crazy-making.

They Create Drama

CNs get energy from drama. They create it when it doesn't need to be there. They are not interested in promoting harmony or peace. They like to do things to keep you rattled, trying to get you to become unglued. They do this by initiating gossip, planting seeds in someone else's ears to direct them to think differently about you. Some CNs will even reach out to your friends or family to try to convince them that you are at fault, unstable, a liar and manipulator, extending their projections to others hoping to drain you of your emotional support. They will send you a rage-filled email or text out of the blue to get a rise out of you. They will have one of their flying monkeys make a passive-aggressive comment on a post you made online. They will subscribe to your YouTube channel or follow you on Instagram or Snapchat to let you know they are still watching you. It's downright creepy.

Some CNs will take you to court, mediation, or an arbitrator as much as they possibly can. It's strange how much time and energy they spend on trying to make your life as miserable as possible. This will still happen to some survivors years after a separation or divorce. Ironically, many CNs will talk about how they hate drama. They will put others down for being dramatic, even telling others how dramatic you are. Be aware that this is yet another projection.

CNs also have a remarkable way of acting completely innocent as they bring pain to others through causing confusion and dissension.

They Don't Make Love; They Take It

I have yet to hear a survivor say sex with a narcissist felt like love. Not all sexual experiences look the same among victims, but they all have the same theme. It's all about the CN. Sex is supposed to be a beautiful bonding experience where both people feel loved and cherished. It is a way of expressing your love for your partner, a chance to give each other pleasure and enjoy each other. Just like a relationship with a CN, sex with them is a one-sided experience.

There is so much to say about this topic that I have dedicated all of chapter eight to it. I spoke with many women and men who found this area of their relationship to be confusing and damaging. It is important to talk about it because there is so much shame involved, yet most survivors stay quiet because of the embarrassment they feel.

They Are Not Protective

A CN cares more about what others think than protecting you. Some men and women have that beautiful protective quality for their loved ones. This is absent with a CN.

If someone criticizes you, a CN won't come to your defense. They will either stay quiet or in passive-aggressive ways suggest to you the criticism might be correct. When you defend yourself, the CN will tell you things such as, *"You are not open to people's opinions," "You are stubborn," "You can't handle the truth,"* etc.

Often a CN will stay quiet when someone hurts you, which makes you question yourself. Many survivors with whom I spoke said they felt emotionally unprotected by these people; they felt alone in these relationships.

Sherry had an experience where someone was verbally abusive to her. She was understandably upset. Her CN husband was there and did nothing to defend her. Instead, they went out to dinner with a group of people that included the man who had been verbally abusive. Sherry felt completely uncomfortable. Her CN knew this and talked to the other people at dinner, including the abuser, as if nothing had happened. Without saying it, her husband gave her clear messages that she was not worthy of respect and kindness, her feelings didn't matter, and she was alone in the relationship.

They Create Stories in Their Head

CNs will tell you mind-boggling stories that have no basis in reality. They will create these tales and accuse you of things that are not even close to the truth. They will presume to know exactly what you are thinking and your motives behind your actions. Because for so long we think of them as being normal and loving us as we loved them, it is a strange thing to witness your spouse or parent not knowing who you are and not having an accurate picture of someone they have lived with for years, sometimes decades.

Torrey was excited when she saw how far she had come as she looked at her CN ex-spouse at a local event. She had felt a lot of anxiety leading up to the day knowing she would see him. She hadn't seen him for years and had always felt weak, flustered, and angry in his presence since the divorce. At first, she was rattled at the sight of him, but as time passed, she found herself actually feeling love for him. After all the cruelty she had experienced, she was surprised and pleased to feel that way. She had done a lot of healing work on herself and felt relieved to see herself not being as affected as she had been in the past. When he came up to her she decided to go with this feeling, so she hugged him and said: *"I love you."* It came from a place of healing—a recognition that she really had loved him and the higher part of her felt a pure love even still. She knew she could never be with him and needed to continue no contact overall. However, in that moment, she decided to just let him be on his own journey and allow herself to feel that divine ever-present love inside of her. Later he wrote her and told her how disgusted he was at her for putting on a show, for acting kind in order to impress people around them. He accused her of being fake and wanting attention. Do you see the projection there? CNs wholeheartedly believe the stories they create in their minds and leave you perpetually blurting out, *"What?!"*

They Have No Desire to Know You

Pretending to want to get to know you is part of grooming you to be their supply. It is not genuine. It is an act of manipulation. As time passes, this becomes more evident. They are not interested in who you are, what you think, and what you feel. This is not a normal, healthy person.

They Have No Interest in Making This a Great Relationship

CNs are not people who fight for relationships or put much work into them at all. Most survivors say they were the ones planning dates, initiating communication, and trying to nurture the relationship. If there are issues in the marriage or partnership, CNs are not the ones to try to find solutions and work through things to come back together. They have no interest in putting effort into relationships.

Control and Manipulation

Covert narcissists control and devalue victims through very subtle manipulation tactics over a long period of time. The impact this has on you is devastating. With each year that you are with the CN, you find yourself feeling less energy, less excitement for life, less confidence, and less joy. You feel like you exist but are not fully alive. You feel yourself slowly declining but aren't sure why. The life in you has been drained.

It's like the story of the frog. If you put a frog in boiling water, it will die a quick and painful death. If you put the frog in lukewarm water and slowly turn up the heat over a long period of time, the frog will eventually die without noticing what is happening. This is what it is like to live with a CN. Your essence, your spirit, the light inside you slowly drains out of you without you noticing. You feel depressed and unmotivated, but you attribute how you are feeling to other things, often blaming yourself for things that are not actually your fault.

We are all aware of the term *manipulation*, but we don't often recognize it when it is happening to us because we don't know what the different tactics that are being used to confuse and control us look like. In the next chapter, I will go into detailed explanations of different ways covert narcissists manipulate so you can see what this looks like in real life and be able to recognize their passive-aggressive behavior.

5
Control and Manipulation Tactics

"Covert emotional manipulation tactics are underhanded methods of control. These deceptive tactics act to change your behavior and perceptions. Covert manipulation operates under the level of your conscious awareness. Victims usually do not realize they are being manipulated while it's happening" (Adelyn Birch, *30 Covert Emotional Manipulation Tactics*).

We rarely see manipulation as it's happening. It operates under the level of our conscious awareness, so it is imperative that we educate ourselves so we can recognize the tactics. It is for this reason I have dedicated an entire chapter to control and manipulation.

The biggest indicator that someone is manipulating you is how you feel around that person. When you are with someone with pure intentions, you feel good about yourself. You feel strong. When you are being manipulated, you doubt yourself, you feel small, you see them as knowing more than you, and you feel mystified and out of sorts. These are red flags.

The good news is the more you educate yourself, the faster you will recognize manipulative behavior, and that recognition is incredibly empowering. You will feel so much stronger and less afraid of life and those around you. You will trust yourself more than ever, and that is a wonderful place to be and live from.

Here are some ways CNs manipulate.

Gaslighting

Gaslighting is a form of manipulation that attempts to grow seeds of doubt in a target. It is used to make you question your memory, your perception, and your own sanity. It makes you think something is wrong with you when it is not. Psychology Today defines gaslighting as, *"A tactic in which a person or entity, in order to gain more power, makes a victim question their reality."*

CNs will accomplish this by using persistent denial, deflection, lying, and blame. The purpose of this is to destabilize you. This keeps you in a weakened state so the CN can control you. You start doubting yourself instead of being able to see the truth of what is happening.

The messages you receive when someone gaslights you are, *"They are always right"* and *"You cannot trust yourself."* If CNs can get you to doubt yourself, they have you under their control. This can last for years, even decades. This tactic makes it difficult to trust your own judgment, beliefs, and instincts. It takes away your confidence. This eventually leads you to depression, forgetting the person you used to be, the carefree spirit who was full of life.

Many victims begin to doubt their own memories. This makes them susceptible to the covert narcissist's opinion. The CN wants to look like they know more than their target, so the target will end up trusting the CN more than them self.

Mark was all too familiar with this tactic. When he would mention stories of events that happened in the past, his CN wife would say, *"That didn't happen."* He was sure it did, but felt confused. Then she would say, *"Who are you going to believe, you with the bad memory or me with the good one?"* This went on for 20 years, making Mark question his memory and his sanity.

Making you doubt your memory is common with gaslighting. One woman I spoke with said she actually made appointments with neurologists because she thought something was seriously wrong with her brain. Some CNs will go to extreme measures, like putting your purse in another room just to make you think you're losing it because you were sure you hung it up in your usual spot.

Gaslighting is subtle, insidious, and intentional, always making you feel like something is wrong with you. When Dawn and Brad were intimate, she told him she felt used after having sex with him and couldn't figure out why because they had such a great relationship. He never addressed how she felt, never looked at himself to see if there were something he might be doing that would make her feel that way. Instead, what he did was direct her attention to things she might need to change about herself. He also told her she was too sensitive and was reading into things. He distracted her, redirecting the focus onto her so she would doubt herself and not notice his deflection. This planted seeds in her mind that Brad would sow for years to come, making her think there was something wrong with her.

In Dawn's case, you can see how Brad did not address her concern, but instead redirected her to think something was wrong with *her.* He kept planting those seeds, watering them as often as he could. He was able to gaslight her for years.

If you find yourself withholding information from your friends and family because of embarrassment or shame, someone might be gaslighting you. After years of not having an orgasm, Dawn never told her friends because of shame, believing something was wrong with her just as Mark never told anyone about the concerns he had with his memory. He fully believed there was something wrong with him.

If you feel hopeless, joyless, bewildered, if you second-guess yourself a lot and question whether you are too sensitive, you might be a victim of gaslighting. If you can't figure out why you are so unhappy when you have so much good in your life, you might be experiencing this type of manipulation. Maybe you find yourself making excuses for your parent or partner's behavior to friends and family. These are all signs you might be experiencing gaslighting.

Triangulation

Triangulation is a manipulative tactic where the CN acts as a messenger between two people. The CN pits the others against each other without either of them noticing that the CN is the one creating the drama. Often, CNs will talk about how they hate drama and put others down for being "so dramatic." The truth is that CNs create drama, but they do so in such a covert way the victims don't notice.

For instance, a CN might lie and tell a neighbor negative things you have been saying about them (when you haven't said anything). Then the CN will come to you and tell you things the neighbor has been saying about you (which the neighbor never said). The CN will word things and play on emotions in such a way that both of you feel badly for the CN having to deal with the stress of this made-up rivalry. Every time you and the neighbor see each other, you both feel anger, hurt, and tension. This can build up over time as the CN keeps stoking the fire by continuing to feed both parties false information about each other. While this is happening, the CN will sit back and watch the animosity grow, maintaining his or her innocent reputation. To your face and the neighbor's, they will act caring and empathetic to your plight. This can go on for years.

After a year of dating, Don told his wife Jackie that his sister said Jackie was a bad driver after she had spent the day taking her around to different sights while she was in town visiting. *"Really?"* Jackie thought that was a strange thing to say. She knew she was a good driver and it seemed like she and Don's sister had a great day together.

"Yes, she also said you made her make your bed while you sat and read a magazine. Is that true? Did you?" Don asked with an innocent look on his face.

"What? No! I would never do that! Why would she say that?"

"I don't know," Don continued. He said it with an innocent tone as if he felt badly for Jackie. It appeared to her that he was on her side.

She was confused. She kept thinking about what he had said and thought,

> *Did I drive recklessly? Did I make her make my bed while I read a magazine? I would never do that! Did I do something that made her feel I wanted her to make my bed? There must be a reason she said all that.*

Jackie questioned her own reality. She was also devastated. She wanted so much for Don's family to like her.

Don later told Jackie she should maybe try harder with his family. She felt so much pressure and hurt. Over the next several years, she worked hard to connect with his family and let them see who she really was, hoping they would like her. At times things seemed good, but then Don would tell her something else a family member said about her. This kept tensions building and made Jackie feel on edge and insecure around his family. This tactic keeps targets distracted, attributing their pain to others instead of revealing the real mastermind behind all of it. It also keeps targets in endless confusion, and they never feel like they're good enough.

The more insecure you are, the more in control CNs are.

If someone is talking badly about his wife, a healthy husband stands up for her and keeps it from her because he knows it will only cause her pain. That's the last thing he wants her to feel because he loves her. I mention this to demonstrate what real love looks like compared to a CN triangulating.

Triangulation can also look like the CN telling his girlfriend about a woman at work who keeps flirting with him. This creates an illusion of him being desirable and instills the fear of her possibly being replaced someday. Emotionally healthy people do not invoke feelings of jealousy and insecurity in people they love.

Another tactic is where a CN will tell his new girlfriend stories of how terrible his ex was to him, how hurtful and difficult she was, how dramatic she was, how crazy she was. Two things happen here. The new girlfriend feels sorry for him, wanting to console him and give him all her attention. The second thing that happens is the CN has now given her subtle messages of how she must behave for him to want her and stay with her. She will live out their relationship making sure she never does or says what his ex used to do and say. This is a way of controlling her behavior.

This tactic emerges again in the discard phase, when the CN has decided he or she doesn't want to be with you anymore. Instead of talking to you about it, they will go to a third party, someone whom they know will agree with them. The CN will often confide in people who barely know you. Then he or she will make sure you know they have been confiding in someone else and that this person agrees that everything is your fault and they should leave you.

After they find another target, the CN talks openly about how much happier they are with their new partner, which is another picture of triangulation.

CNs do not respect you. They do not care about your feelings. They have a lot of rage and no empathy. They only care about themselves. This is the bottom line.

Intermittent Reinforcement

Intermittent reinforcement in the context of a relationship is when kindness and loving acts are not given consistently, but rather intermittently. In *30 Covert Emotional Manipulation Tactics*, author Adelyn Birch writes, *"This is an extremely powerful and effective manipulation tactic. In fact, psychology experts consider it the most powerful motivator in existence."*

Intermittent reinforcement is a conditioning behavior where CNs set the rules. Their love is inconsistent and on their terms. This leaves you feeling unstable and longing for their love and attention. The relationship becomes a mixture of subtle cruelty and periodic affection. They will woo you and withhold from you.

This conditions you to keep trying to please them in order to get the reward of love. It brings you to a place where you lower your standards so much that you become grateful for mediocre treatment that you never would have tolerated when you first met them. You end up believing you don't deserve any better and that you are not worthy of love and affection. Or you think this is just what happens in marriages. In dating situations, CNs will seem uncertain about you and other times they will express how you are the only one for them. You never know where you stand with them.

Dr. Robert Sapolsky, a neuroendocrinologist and author, does a great job explaining on a YouTube video why intermittent reinforcement is such a powerful and effective manipulative tool. (The link is under Educational Resources at the back of this book.) I highly recommend it. He explains what happened to dopamine levels in monkeys when the reinforcement patterns changed during a study that was published a little more than a decade ago. The monkeys were trained to learn that when a light went on, if they pressed the lever, they would receive a reward. They were rewarded every time. Dopamine levels didn't rise when they got the reward. Instead, they rose in anticipation of the reward coming.

Then the scientists changed the rules. The monkeys did the same amount of work, but only got rewards half the time, and the rewards were handed out unpredictably. What do you think happened to the dopamine levels? They rose to levels similar to when someone uses cocaine. This is what happens to the brain when you introduce "maybe" into the equation. It is an incredibly powerful control tactic. People will work like mad for a "maybe" far more than they will for certainty. In the video Sapolsky notes, *"You never get more behavior out of an organism than when you have introduced a maybe into it."*

Do you see the parallels? The monkeys were experiencing love bombing in the beginning. When the rules changed, this began the devaluing stage. This is why the love-bombing stage is so powerful—it sets you up to work incredibly hard to receive intermittent morsels of love. Your brain was literally conditioned by the CN to stay with them because of the powerful hope of "maybe."

A CN will say loving and nice things to you, compliment you, make you dinner, buy you gifts, but only on a random basis. Mixed in with this nice, loving behavior that keeps you thinking this is the person you fell in love with is also belittling that keeps you feeling weak and small, silent treatment that makes you think you've done something wrong, moodiness that makes you believe you are the source of their unhappiness, and several other means of making you feel insecure and not good enough.

You will feel your CN withdraw at times, which makes you worry and sends your brain spinning into all kinds of anxious thoughts. *"Did I say something wrong? Did I do something I shouldn't have?"* You will expend a lot of energy trying to bring them back to you, trying to undo whatever you might have done. Then they will be kind to you, and you'll feel relief. It's an emotional rollercoaster run off their moods, and it keeps you constantly giving them attention. As long as you are doing this, you are useful to them as their energy supply. This keeps you off-kilter and susceptible to manipulation and control.

It makes you feel desperate, dependent on their attention, working hard for a reward of love and attention that only comes on their terms, intermittently, and unpredictably. Many times victims think they are codependent because they act in ways that a codependent does, but the truth is that many victims I've met are not codependent. They have been manipulated in such a way that they behave in ways they normally wouldn't. When they get out of these relationships and begin to see things clearly, they come back to themselves, and in fact become a much stronger version of their previous self.

The False Apology

When you research narcissism, often you hear people say narcissists never apologize. Frequently, that is true of an overt narcissist, but it can be a different story with a CN.

When Joanne met her husband and continuing for the first few years of their marriage, she was so impressed by how easily and quickly he apologized. He was better than her at apologizing, better than anyone she knew, really. Looking back, she noticed a pattern of him listening to her express how something he did or said hurt her, then apologizing, then changing his behavior for a couple days, then repeating the same old behavior. After a while, with all the other responsibilities of life, she stopped trying; she learned to just accept things about him that weren't ideal and enjoy the good parts. He wore her down and subtly taught her it wasn't worth the effort to confront him and tell him her feelings.

CNs don't have empathy, but they know how to act like they do. The same goes for apologies. They can be very adept at saying they are sorry without actually meaning it. They appease you for the time being, but have no interest in changing to improve the relationship or treat you better.

Deflecting the Focus

CNs have a way of turning things around and making something your fault. They will emotionally wound you; then you will confront them about it. They will somehow end up making you feel badly about something, and you find yourself apologizing to them even though they were the one who hurt you. This is a common pattern victims experience.

Claire kept receiving abusive emails from her CN after they divorced. She ignored them for a while as she tried to have no contact. Then one day she decided to stand up for herself and say something. She wrote him back and said if he sent more emotionally abusive emails, she would have to block him. Her email was brief and to the point. He responded within a few hours with a two-page essay telling her that what she considers abuse is actually the truth about what is wrong with her that she is not willing to face. He told her she couldn't handle people being honest with her. He went on, in a cruel and abusive way, to list several other things that were "wrong" with her. They are big fans of deflecting the focus off them and onto you, making themselves the victims and blaming you for all kinds of things that are massive distortions of reality.

I have seen this happen in spiritual circles as well as self-improvement conferences. Kevin, a spiritual leader at a healing center in Costa Rica, would speak to the female attendees in inappropriate ways. They felt uncomfortable around him. When one woman confronted him about his inappropriate behavior, he put the focus back on her by saying in a gentle voice, *"It sounds like you are being triggered, Sara. What is this bringing up for you?"* He acted like it was a learning experience for her instead of owning up to his actions and taking responsibility. This left her confused about what just happened, especially because he was the revered leader; he sounded so kind and caring. By deflecting the attention onto her, he kept his status as the revered leader, and she left feeling like there was something wrong with her that she needed to fix. This also left her with the harmful message that it was okay for a man to treat her in a demeaning and disrespectful way.

Blame

CNs blame their victims for anything and everything. One of their ways of controlling is taking no personal responsibility and putting the fault on you for their bad behavior.

- *"I'm being verbally abusive to you because you set the tone when you hired an attorney, so it's your fault I'm abusive."*
- *"I had an affair because you wouldn't get a Brazilian wax when I told you how much it would mean to me. It showed me how much you didn't care about me. You made me have an affair."*
- *"I had to close the bank accounts because you bought a new washing machine when the old one broke without asking."*

Here are some statements I've heard targets say they have heard from their CN:

- *"It's your fault the kids don't like me."*
- *"It's your fault I was never happy."*
- *"It's your fault my family didn't like you."*
- *It's your fault I'm unhappy every Christmas. If you would enjoy the process of decorating the tree instead of rushing through it, I would enjoy Christmas more."*

- *"It's your fault our son didn't get into Northwestern."*
- *"It's your fault I am emotionally shut down."*
- *"It's your fault our daughter never played softball."*
- *"It's your fault I watch porn."*
- *"It's your fault I'm irritable."*
- *"It's your fault I don't have friends."*
- *"It's your fault we are in debt."*
- *"It's your fault I'm depressed and angry."*
- *"It's your fault I abuse you."*
- *And the grand finale… "You blame me for everything because you won't take any personal responsibility."*

Distorting Reality

CNs will throw strong statements at you that make no sense and have no basis in reality, but they speak in such a strong and convincing way it makes you consider things that are obviously false. Their accusations of you are almost as ludicrous as them saying you alone are responsible for the lack of affordable health care or the ice caps melting, and you take a moment to wonder if they are right. You do this because you have been manipulated for a very long time. You have been brainwashed, and that takes time to unravel.

The accusations they will throw at you keep you spinning inside. You end up expending a lot of energy around these ridiculous statements because you have a hard time believing this person, whom you loved and trusted, is lying to you and manipulating you. It takes time to undo years of illusion and see the truth. It will happen. You will see clearly, it will just take some time. You're going to be fine, better than you can probably imagine right now.

Mary's story illustrates what it looks like for a CN to distort reality. Her CN ex-husband tried to drain her of money every chance he could. One day their daughter wanted financial help with a trip she was taking. Mary didn't receive any child support for her as her CN had petitioned early on to take that away from her. Her CN told their daughter he would give her a certain amount if Mary matched it (using children is another common form of triangulation). He had much more money than Mary, and this put Mary in a position to give a lot of money she didn't have. She agreed to a lesser amount, thinking if he didn't agree she would come up with some way to help her daughter, but she didn't want to give in to his demands, letting him order her around as he would so often do. She was working on being stronger with him and setting boundaries for how he can and can't treat her. She wrote him and told him how much she could pay.

He replied immediately with a rage-filled email telling her what a horrible mom she was and how selfish and materialistic she was. He made dramatic statements about her neglect of their daughter, followed by, *"It's like you've washed your hands of her!"* She read that sentence while sitting in her bedroom. She looked up from her computer at their daughter's room across the hall and saw the shorts lying on her bed Mary had just bought her. She thought about the oil change she just paid for their daughter's car, all the hours she spent with their daughter helping her figure out her life, all the hugs, all the meals she made her, the stocked fridge, how she made sure her favorite foods were there. She thought, *Yeah, that sounds about right…This is definitely a picture of a woman who has washed her hands of her daughter.*

This was not only a distortion of reality, but also a projection of what was true of him. The truth was this man was out of touch with their daughter, barely saw her, and sadly made very little effort to be involved in her life.

I have heard so many other stories like this from victims with whom I've spoken. They are amazing moms and dads who truly love their kids and take incredible care of them when the CN doesn't, but the CN paints the opposite picture. It is deplorable how targets are treated by CNs who continuously criticize their parenting. Sadly, it is common for CNs to use their children to get back at the victim.

Indirect Insults/Insinuating Comments

CNs are rarely direct with their insults until the discard phase. Instead, they will phrase belittling, degrading, and disrespectful comments in a way that makes you wonder, *Was that a putdown? It sounded like a putdown. It felt terrible. But they are looking at me with an innocent look on their face that makes me completely dumbfounded.*

Sue went on a family vacation with her CN husband, Stuart, and their two kids. Their kids wanted to eat breakfast at the all-you-can-eat buffet in the restaurant at the resort. Since it was expensive, Sue told them they would have one special morning where they could all eat there. The day finally came. Stuart was being difficult on the vacation—moody and irritable as usual—so Sue got up early that morning to have some quiet time by herself before the rest of the family woke. She texted them that she'd be down at the restaurant and they could meet her there when they were ready to eat. She thought she'd get some coffee and journal while she waited for the three of them.

The kids came running, excited to eat this massive array of food, followed by their CN dad. They walked up to the table where

Sue was sitting with her coffee. Stuart looked at Sue and said with a cheery, innocent tone, *"Oh, you came down here and ate the buffet by yourself?"* Their kids looked at him strangely as there were no plates at her table. Their daughter gave her dad a confused look and said, *"Like mom would ever do that…"*

To the average person, this may not seem like a big deal. But anyone who has lived with a CN knows these little-disguised digs happen a lot, especially toward the end. The CN says something that sounds innocent, but the victim can feel the passive-aggressive putdown behind it.

To continue probing deeper with this couple's example, Sue was roughly 40 pounds overweight. She felt insecure about it, especially on vacation. She was trying to eat better and lose the weight. Stuart knew this. He also knew from 27 years of being in a relationship with Sue that she would never go out to eat by herself. That wasn't her personality. He used her insecurities to hurt her. When he "casually" and "innocently" made a comment about her eating a whole buffet by herself, he was saying much more than the comment itself.

People who haven't experienced covert narcissism might say Sue was reading into this, that he was just asking a question. Stuart would say the same thing, telling Sue how overly sensitive she is, how touchy she is, how high-maintenance she is. This is why many victims are scared to tell their story because sometimes the scenarios don't sound that bad. Like the woman who says her husband spent a lot of time working in the yard and she felt abandoned. Most people would hear that and think she needs to get a hobby. The reality is this woman was picking up on something. She could feel it. She had lived with covert messages of how unworthy she was of her CN's love for years. She had experienced many subtle ways he would "punish" her for not being the way he wanted her to be.

It is insidious abuse because no one sees it, but the victim feels it profoundly. It affects every fiber of their being.

Mixed Messages

Radically contrasting messages are some of the most bizarre aspects of life with a CN.

Let's go back to another example from an earlier couple. Throughout Sara's 15-year marriage to Bill, he would tell her he wanted her to go after her dreams and be the artist she had always wanted to be. He said he made enough money, so she didn't have to work. She felt incredibly lucky to have such a generous and supportive husband. She spent their married life raising their kids and pursuing her art. During the discard phase, Bill told her she should have been working the whole time. He said she only married him for his money and never really cared about him.

For years, Callie's husband told her how beautiful her body was, then when he was done with her, he said, *"Maybe I should have been harder on you so you would have lost the weight. I let you eat whatever you wanted."*

Every birthday, Sam would say he didn't need anything, not to make a fuss over him. Scott, his partner, would still always make it nice for him, really thinking about what he would love to experience and what kind of thoughtful gift he could buy him. They were tight on money one year, so Scott got creative with gift-giving and planning Sam's special day, still making it very heartfelt. After his birthday, Sam was sulking, moody, and grumpy. His partner asked him what was wrong. After several circular conversations, Sam yelled, *"I thought you were going to get me an iPad!"* His partner was completely baffled. He hadn't said a word about wanting an iPad, something that was way out of their budget anyway. Even so, Scott found himself feeling bad, as if he had done something terribly wrong. When they broke up, Sam told Scott he wanted someone more spiritual, that Scott was way too materialistic for him.

Sometimes CNs will send you an email or phone message that is incredibly loving and kind. Then a few hours later, they will tell you what a horrible person you are. Relationships with CNs are filled with destructive mixed messages.

Punishing

CNs often use passive-aggressive means to punish you when you do not behave in ways they want. Sometimes they will give you the silent treatment, act as if they didn't hear you, or be distant when you long for connection. They will pull away and starve you of attention and affection. They will do things to inconvenience you, disrupting your life in some way.

CNs often will use money as a tool to punish you by hiding assets and cutting off your financial supply, sometimes controlling every dime you spend. They will leave you to handle everything after they move out, taking care of the kids, selling the home, moving everything on your own, getting rid of things, taking care of bills, etc.

CNs consistently will "forget" to pick up an item at the store that you had asked them to get on their way home. They will "forget" things that then fall in your lap to handle. These instances are usually followed by a false apology made to appease you.

CNs despise helping you when you are sick or in need of care, so they will subtly punish you during these times. Rebecca's dad would become even more distant, moody, and angry when Rebecca got sick. She felt as if her dad was mad at her for not feeling well. He would make a big deal if he did anything to help his daughter and gave the clear message she was a huge burden without saying that directly to her.

When Susan had surgery, her CN husband, Harry, brought her home from the hospital. She was still coming out of the effects of anesthesia when he sat at her bedside and confronted her about her "bad behavior." He told her she didn't seem very appreciative of his help at the hospital when she was waking up. He needed more from her than that, he said. She could barely focus on what he was saying as he was telling her about his hurt feelings. Susan felt confused and stressed, not to mention in pain. She had no energy to respond. He made sure to not be around a lot during her recovery. She was on her own to heal *and* take care of the kids.

CNs will punish you with their moods. You might have saved up for a concert that excites you. The CN comes with you and is irritable the whole time, making it hard for you to enjoy it.

CNs will punish you by withholding attention, not complimenting you when you have dressed up for a date with them, invalidating your feelings, not defending you when someone else treats you badly, smearing your name to others, trying to turn your kids against you, offering subtle putdowns, and using your insecurities and personal things you have opened up to them about to wound you. Years of this treatment slowly breaks down your spirit, the life inside you. You lose track of what a loving relationship looks like and, tragically, you begin to believe you don't deserve any better.

Minimization

A CN will minimize your painful experience with them, which makes you doubt and question your own feelings and reality. Dr. George K. Simon, Jr. describes this form of manipulation in his book, *In Sheep's Clothing*:

> *"This tactic is a unique kind of denial coupled with rationalization. When using this maneuver, the aggressor is attempting to assert that his behavior isn't really as harmful or irresponsible as someone else may be claiming."*

Many victims wonder if they are blowing things out of proportion, thinking their ex or parent or coworker is a CN. Women I talked to wonder if they are to blame and the CN was actually a great love who they will regret leaving. Many wonder if they, themselves, are narcissists. CNs will use your doubts against you, saying you are overly dramatic, too sensitive, you don't take responsibility for yourself, you blame everyone instead, etc.

The thing to remember is you can trust yourself. Your pain is real. Allow yourself to recognize this. If something feels off, that is because it is.

6

Covert Narcissistic Parents

"You are so lucky to have a dad/mom like yours!" To the outside world, your parent can seem perfect. They appear kind, easy to approach, and speak to others about how much they care for their kids. These are often the moms who write thank-you notes, send sympathy cards, and bring casseroles to neighbors when they are going through a difficult time. They might volunteer at the school. The dad might coach his son or daughter's soccer team; he's the one who is easy to talk to and who everyone loves. In public, he is kind and patient with his kids. The other moms wish their husbands could be that great.

Most children of CN parents don't realize one of their parents is a covert narcissist until they are in their thirties. I've noticed in my interviews that this age is a common time for awakening. It is a painful experience, but also validating.

It is common for children of covert narcissistic parents to hear how lucky they are to have a mom/dad like they do throughout their childhood. This doesn't always happen, but is quite common. This makes things very confusing for the child and invalidates how they feel about their CN parent. I have noticed, though, some differences in CN moms and CN dads. The stories might be different, but the traits are the same, and how they make a child feel is similar. They are incredibly selfish individuals who use their kids as their supply.

CN parents seem to either be overly enmeshed in their kids' lives, or they are the parent who is uninvolved. The parent who is absent or uninvolved will connect with their kids if the conversation centers on a topic of interest to the CN parent. In those moments, the child feels loved, but it doesn't last. The CNs won't engage in what the child needs. They do not know their children and are not aware of their needs. They may know them on a surface level, but don't take the time to really get to know them on a deeper level. They often label their kids as being certain ways that are far from the truth of who their kids actually are. As with all narcissists, they project their own issues onto their children, calling them manipulative, controlling, selfish, and other traits that they possess themselves.

Some CN parents are great with young kids until they reach an age where they think for themselves. That's when the CN dad or mom begins to pull away. They will get more irritated and frustrated with their kids because they (the CNs) are no longer seen as amazing. The kids are no longer supplying their CN parent with adoration and attention like they did when they were younger and would run up to them excitedly yelling, "Daddy!" or "Mommy!" Whether the parent is overly involved or very uninvolved, the impact is the same—there is no help with the development of self from either one. The child feels alone and unseen.

All CNs are selfish at their core, so that is how they are as parents. They want their child's attention and praise. Some CN parents will focus more time and love onto the "golden child" who gives them the most adoration. The CN parent will become frustrated and angry with the child who doesn't want to "get into their world." They will give them the silent treatment and punish them by withdrawing from them. The CN dad or mom will be kinder to the child who will listen to him or her, often the more sensitive, empathetic child who doesn't want any conflict. The other child (or children) will be labeled as controlling, selfish, or manipulative by the parent. The CN may not say things to their children's faces, but they will feel the judgment and dislike from the CN parent.

The "golden child" is lavished on and treated with more kindness. This can seem like a nice thing for this child, but in fact it puts them in the position of trying to be perfect in order to keep that love and attention. They watch as their siblings are treated differently. They naturally want to keep that good feeling of being loved by their mom or dad, so they learn early on how they must behave to be treated with love. This sets them up for a life that is filled with the pressure of never being less than perfect in anything they do. It has been instilled in them that this is how they get people to love them and to keep their love and attention. They also don't expect to be unconditionally loved, so often they choose partners who don't treat them with consistent, pure love. They never feel good enough and can live with underlying despair and unhappiness for a long time.

Everyone I interviewed was clearly affected by living with a CN. What I noticed is the ones who were married to a CN for more than 20 years physically shook while they told their stories. Their lips quivered. There were lots of tears and confusion. They were shaken like a person who had come back from war where they experienced unspeakable things. They were in shock. They had been traumatized and were trying to make sense of things.

It was different when I talked with adult children of CN parents. There was a quiet feeling of low-level sadness. These were stunning women and men who were suppressed and shut down, like someone who had experienced so much covert abuse that the life in them had been drained over a long period of time. They were tired and emotionally worn out.

My heart broke when I spoke with them. They were all such strong, smart women and men who had been subtly traumatized by someone who was supposed to love them, all the while hearing from their friends how great their covert abuser was or how lucky they were to have a parent like that.

One woman said she hated when her friends would come over because her mom would be so nice to them and they would leave thinking what a great life she had. She was dying inside, and no one could see. For instance, Gail said she didn't like going out with her mom, watching her turn on intoxicating charm that swept others away. She felt jealous and wished she could have that same attention. At home she walked on eggshells, trying to match her mom's emotions because if she succeeded, there would be peace. Her mom would tell her how great a mother she was compared to other parents. As a child, Gail believed that to be true—that her mother was a gift and a treasure to so many people. She seemed perfect in many ways. Gail's mother was a pillar in the community, a volunteer in her church. It wasn't until she was in her mid-thirties that she realized her mom was a covert narcissist.

Christy had a mom who was seen as a great parent by others as well. At home her mom would have extravagant decorations every Christmas, but it always felt like she did it to impress their friends and neighbors. As Christy got older, her mom stopped decorating and complained about how much she hated the holidays. Christy ended up doing all the decorating herself and was shamed by her mother for liking Christmas. Also, her birthdays were either completely uneventful, or a big extravagant party to impress others, and her mom made it all about her rather than Christy. After her college graduation ceremony, Christy came home to find a large, beautifully wrapped box waiting for her. Excited, she opened it only to find lime-green towels and a set of white plastic hangers. Her heart sank. Even though she had experienced years of disappointing gifts that showed her mom didn't know her and didn't care, there was still a glimmer of hope that this time might be different, that the gift would be some sign her mom really did care about her and wanted to give her something really special on her big day. Christy had hoped to find something wonderful in the box, something truly meaningful, and at the same time she felt ashamed for her ungratefulness. She smiled and said "thank you" to her mom.

When you live with a covert narcissist, it is common to feel let down, followed by shame for not being appreciative. There is also that hope that the person you believed loved you and should know you better than anyone else might come through for you.

Christy told me she felt like she had lived with an enduring low-level sadness her whole life. I felt this from her, and my heart broke. She is kind, caring, real, honest, smart, and tender; she deserves so much better. Many adult daughters of CN mothers told me stories about growing up, stories of confusion, cruelty, and manipulation, mixed with loving statements. The majority of them said they considered their mom to be their best friend until they were well into adulthood.

Allie's mom praised her constantly. She was very involved in her life. She would make sure she excelled in school, to the point that she would redo a lot of her projects to make sure they would be impressive and get high grades. She would get all the books and supplies Allie needed. Her mom was frequently stressed, so Allie even made sure she cleaned and did helpful things around the house to help her. This resulted in her growing up feeling on edge. She felt responsible for her mom's anxiety, believing she was to blame. If she didn't exist, her mom would be happier, she reasoned. Mom CNs often act like martyrs. Allie's mom would do normal mom things, such as make dinner, but would make a big deal of it, causing Allie to feel a lot of guilt. There is intense underlying manipulation that makes children feel so much guilt and shame. They blame themselves a lot and feel like they are responsible for how their CN parent feels.

CN parents are also very out of touch with their kids. They will tell others how their kids are doing, usually sharing glowing reports that are not based in reality. *"Tommy's doing great!"* they'll say to friends when the truth is Tommy keeps missing school because he is experiencing depression.

I've heard kids of CN dads say it feels to them like he acts like he's listening, but he is not really there, he doesn't really hear them. What they say just seems to bounce off him instead of penetrating his heart and mind. He acts like he cares, but it doesn't really feel like he does. It's not a normal back-and-forth exchange with CN parents. It is an act and almost feels scripted. It is impossible to have a deep, authentic connection with a CN parent.

Many times when CN parents give life advice to their kids, it leaves the kids feeling badly about themselves and questioning their own decisions, their own thinking. Oftentimes CN parents will set up their kids to think they won't be able to handle life on their own, so the children form an unhealthy dependency. One woman noticed that every time her son came back from visiting his CN dad he would be more down on himself, more scared of life, and would express thoughts of feeling lazy. The son never noticed the link that these thoughts only happened after seeing his dad because the manipulation was so subtle. He never heard his dad say he was lazy or incapable, but somehow he felt that after being with him. His dad's life advice left him feeling overwhelmed and fearful, not believing he had what it takes to survive out there on his own.

Rhonda's mom used a different tactic and kept Rhonda very sheltered. She had strict rules for her. Her mom would talk about all the evil people in the world and that Rhonda needed to be alert. She kept Rhonda close at her side. This gave Rhonda an unhealthy dependency on her mom, as well as instilled a great fear of anything outside her home. Rhonda is in her forties now and still struggles with trusting her own decision-making ability. Her mom still belittles her and tells her how "concerned" she is about choices Rhonda is making.

"Have you thought about this, Rhonda? I'm just really concerned that you're going to get hurt. I can tell you don't know exactly what you're doing. Can I fix your hair for you? It would look so much nicer if you grew it out."

Rhonda told me her mom would give her *"compliments laced with shit."*

A common theme I have seen with children of CN parents is it is hard for them to believe in themselves. They doubt their own capabilities. Often a CN parent will make them feel terrible about themselves when they give them advice, but act as if they care and are concerned. The children feel downtrodden, discouraged, stressed, and confused. It is hard for them to think clearly and feel any strength around their CN parent.

Autumn discovered a strange thing when she met other daughters of CN moms—she couldn't believe they all had the same bizarre memory in common. She remembers her mom often singing a certain song around the house. The song is from the musical *Annie Get Your Gun*, with one round of lyrics stating, *"Anything you can do I can do better. I can do anything better than you."* She shared this with other women in a support group. They couldn't believe it—their moms used to walk around their house singing the same song.

Some CN moms get jealous of their children. They are emotionally immature and extraordinarily selfish. They will encourage their child with a project the child chooses, but then when the child starts to succeed, the mom will cultivate seeds of doubt in their mind. These won't be obvious, but the child will feel discouraged and begin to question them self.

CN parents act as if they care, but don't have the empathy to really care as someone would who is genuine and compassionate. Unconditional, selfless love does not exist with a CN parent.

I asked different women and men how they felt when they were around their CN moms or dads growing up. Here are some things they said:

- *"I felt under stress a lot."*
- *"I felt very apprehensive."*
- *"I was hyper-aware of Mom's mood changes."*
- *"I felt like I was on edge, waiting to know how to feel."*
- *"I second-guessed myself a lot."*
- *"It had to be his idea, or he would make me pay."*
- *"I didn't feel like I was allowed to think bad thoughts about my mom."*

- *"I felt tense a lot."*
- *"Money was always a stressful topic."*
- *"If I did well in school she would tell me it was because of her because she sat next to me and helped me study."*
- *"I often had headaches and a tight neck."*
- *"I felt a lot of anxiety."*
- *"I felt like I was walking on eggshells, never knowing what would set him off."*
- *"I felt like there was no way I could win and have his full approval."*
- *"I felt depressed a lot."*
- *"I felt like a showpiece."*
- *"I never felt good enough."*
- *"I felt like everything was always my fault."*
- *"I felt embarrassed."*
- *"I was scared to speak up and say what I really thought."*
- *"I felt constantly judged."*
- *"I felt like I would never make it in life without her."*
- *"I felt confined, suffocated."*
- *"I felt like I was starving for a self-identity."*
- *"He controlled me through his emotions."*
- *"I felt deeply guilty when my mom was upset. I felt like it was my fault."*
- *"I felt responsible for her feelings."*
- *"I felt responsible to make her feel better."*
- *"I felt small and weak."*
- *"I felt dependent on her."*
- *"I didn't feel like I could be my own independent person."*
- *"All of his unresolved baggage became mine."*
- *"She did not want me to leave the house or have friends over."*
- *"My parents raised me to be dependent on them."*

- *"I felt like I owed her for being my mom."*
- *"I felt like I needed to thank her profusely for every little thing."*
- *"I felt belittled."*
- *"There were happy, fun times, but I could never relax knowing her mood could change at any moment."*
- *"He never defended me or stood up for me."*
- *"I felt like I never knew as much as him."*
- *"I learned not to trust my own decision making."*
- *"He had a shallow view of who I was, but never really knew me."*
- *"I felt like I should be grateful for my mom because her childhood was worse. I didn't feel like it was okay to feel my own sadness."*
- *"I couldn't win, no matter how good and kind I was."*
- *"My childhood felt like soul rape."*

To see the contrast, when I asked them how other people would describe their CN mom or dad these were the answers I heard:

- *"She's so nice."*
- *"She understands people and really cares."*
- *"She's very charismatic."*
- *"She's so helpful."*
- *"He is so kind."*
- *"He is so patient."*
- *"He is such a good listener."*
- *"She is so loving."*
- *"She is great mom and wife."*
- *"He's such a great dad."*
- *"He's so laid-back and easy to be around."*

I also asked them what messages they received from their CN parent about themselves, whether they said them directly or covertly through their looks, actions, and manipulative talk. Here are some of the messages:

- *"You are not worthy of being taken care of."*
- *"You are fat."*
- *"You are lazy."*
- *"You are sloppy."*
- *"You're not as good as me."*
- *"You're not as smart as me."*
- *"You ruined my life, and you need to atone for it."*
- *"You are responsible for my happiness."*
- *"You are beautiful, smart, and lazy."*
- *"You have all this wonderful stuff, but you don't use it."*
- *"You can't trust yourself."*
- *"You will never be as perfect as me."*
- *"I know more than you and always will."*
- *"You can't do anything on your own."*
- *"You are only wanted when you are nice. No one will want all of you."*
- *"You are weak."*
- *"You are too sensitive."*
- *"You are too soft-hearted."*
- *"You are annoying."*
- *"You're pretty."*
- *"You can do anything."*
- *"No matter how perfect you are, you will never be enough."*

When I asked one woman what messages she got from her CN mom, she said, *"You are so beautiful, you are better than all the other kids, and you are shit."* This is an accurate picture of what it is like to grow up with a CN parent, experiencing intermittent reinforcement and destructive mixed messages for years while you are forming your identity and your view of the world around you. Words and actions that appear loving contrasted with demeaning and devaluing messages, whether straightforward or subtle.

CN parents often will manipulate their kids into thinking the healthy parent is the one to blame for everything. They will paint a picture that makes the kids question if they can trust the one who is actually there for them and see the CN parent as the victim.

I spoke with a dad and his daughter recently. After years of seeing him as the inept parent because of her CN mom, she and her dad are now getting to know each other, and it is a beautiful bond to watch. She was raised with a twisted view of her dad from her mom. Now in adulthood, she is beginning to see the truth.

Kids will learn to make excuses for their CN parent's absence and unhealthy behavior. They have never experienced what a healthy dad or mom looks and feels like, so they see their CN parent's behavior as normal since it is all they know. The CN knows just what to say to keep their kids believing their lies and manipulative tactics.

CN parents lie; they are manipulative. They lack empathy and a strong sense of self. They are selfish. They will put other things ahead of their kids, but make it sound as if they have a reasonable excuse for doing so. Their words don't match their actions. They will act like the victim and blame the other parent or the child for things that are in fact true of the CN. They create drama, but act as if they are not the cause of it. They love bomb, devalue, and can discard their kids if the children do not give them the attention they require. However, to the outside, they often look ideal.

Adults who have been raised by a CN parent are deeply wounded and find it difficult to see their profound value. If you have experienced a CN parent, I would love to give you the biggest, warmest hug in the world. You are tender, beautiful, and worth loving. You have been given messages about yourself and life that are not true, and I am so sorry. You deserve so much better than that. I hope this chapter and book help validate things you have experienced and are still experiencing. May you surround yourself with genuine loving people and heal those wounded parts of your heart that deserve love, happiness, and life.

I honor you for your courageous journey.

7

In the Workplace

Covert narcissists tend to be financially successful people. They want to look good to others, and this is all part of the image that is so important to them. Because of this, they can often be found in leadership positions in organizations.

When you start out working with or for these people, they seem like the dream boss, coworker, or partner. You feel incredibly lucky to be working with them. They compliment you and make you feel valued and needed. They are often described as charismatic people, the boss or employee everyone likes.

CN bosses are easy to work with, and many victims feel relieved to have a boss like them after experiencing difficult employers in the past. However, they are often chameleons who mirror the people they are around, so everyone feels like they are seen by them and understood. They win people's trust quickly. They are charming, but not in a creepy-player kind of way. They seem like the real deal. Easygoing, smart, not a big ego, endearing—these are words I have heard to describe this type of person.

As in romantic relationships, a CN boss will take you through the three stages. They will love bomb you in the beginning. It will feel easy, exciting, fun. They might make grandiose promises of your future with the company, your financial success, and your involvement in projects you love. You will feel excited and so lucky to have gotten this opportunity, telling your friends and family all the glowing stories of this new boss. Sometimes this person becomes a trusted friend.

I talked to Tom who became partners with his boss and worked alongside him for years. Trust was built. Their families would get together on the weekends to barbecue by the lake. Their kids became friends. Everyone at the office loved this guy, so when the subtle devaluing began, Tom didn't feel free to talk about it with anyone. He voiced concerns a couple of times to gauge if he was seeing things clearly and the reaction of his coworkers was, *"What are you talking about? You have the greatest boss ever!"* He got the message there was no one he could confide in. He also thought he probably misread something and doubted his own mind and intuition.

Sally had the same story with her boss. After the love-bombing stage, little things started to happen, like how her boss would call her late at night with a crisis at work. She felt like she had to be at his beck and call. He crossed boundaries with acts such as this, and showed Sally he did not respect her. Sally let things slide for years because she had developed a friendship with her boss and believed she could trust him and that he cared about her.

After a time, Sally's boss started bringing up "concerns" he had about her. He would talk about how he knew she had a lot of stress with her ailing parents and wanted to make sure she was okay because she didn't seem to have a great memory, lately. He would sometimes tease her about her memory but passed it off lightly as just being a joke. It wasn't a joke; he was devaluing her, minimizing her pain.

John experienced the same gaslighting from his boss. In fact, his was so extreme he found out later his boss had deleted files, and had not told John about meetings to make John question his own memory. John's health began to decline while he worked there, but he shrugged it off as just stress from working long hours. His boss gaslighted him so much over the years he actually went to see a neurologist to see if something was wrong with his brain. John was convinced his memory was rapidly evaporating and wondered if he had early-onset dementia in his mid-thirties.

You can see how working with a CN boss can deplete you of energy and affect your health in damaging ways.

Another common trait with a CN boss is him or her taking credit for your work and ideas, but doing this in such sneaky, underhanded, charming ways, you feel like a jerk if you mention it. You fear losing your job and learn to keep quiet.

CNs keep you unglued through many different tactics. One of these is minimizing your feelings and pain by doing hurtful things, then when you have a natural reaction, they act innocently or say they were only kidding, or somehow make you feel shame for your organic reaction. They also set you up to look a certain way in front of others to discredit you. Amy said her boss would give her strange gifts, including a book that was offensive. She would react strongly, and he would act innocently, saying, *"Oh my gosh, I'm so sorry. I had no idea that would offend you. I was told it was a popular book."* Other coworkers watching this would think Amy was overly sensitive and started seeing her through those eyes.

Amy's boss would also sabotage her by letting her know about meetings she needed to be at right before they started, knowing she wouldn't be able to make them. Sometimes she would struggle and underperform. He did nothing to help her out and did not seem to care when he saw this happening. Instead, he would add more work for her to do. She started to feel like she was letting him down. Her confidence fell. She believed she was the problem and he let her believe it. She was so affected by her experience that she began to isolate herself more and more from people. She stayed home a lot when she wasn't at work, stopped calling friends to get together. She began to feel unworthy, unlovable, a waste of space.

With all CNs, there is a cognitive dissonance that happens. You have competing beliefs about your boss/friend. They still appear like the person you first "loved," but they also make you feel terrible about yourself. Reconciling this is such a confusing and crazy-making thing for the brain and heart. Working with a CN leaves you feeling exhausted, overwhelmed, and insecure.

Another way they keep the manipulation going is through smear campaigns. Sally's boss would talk to other coworkers about her, and they began to wonder if she had a mental illness. He would share with them how "concerned" he was about her.

Most targets are self-reflective people, so they often look at themselves as possibly being at fault. It is the hardest and most foreign thing in the world to consider that someone who "cares" about you and treats you so well in so many ways is also sabotaging and controlling you. This is not a thought that enters the mind of a trusting, honest, self-reflective person. CN bosses and coworkers greatly affect your self-esteem and your belief in your own intuition and intelligence.

As with other relationships with CNs, there are a lot of mixed messages and intermittent reinforcement. They will make grand gestures; they might defend you in front of others. They will look out for you at times, as well as demean and devalue you. All the nice acts make you question negative thoughts you have about them.

You end up turning on yourself, thinking something is wrong with you. *Why can't I just relax? Why can't I enjoy and appreciate her/him like everyone else seems to?*

Victims are not the only ones affected by CN bosses. I talked to Emma, a mother of two young kids. She missed important events with them because of her boss constantly filling her schedule. Her boss was aware of how important these dates were to her and her family, yet she would add more work and appointments to Emma's schedule during these specific dates. Emma was stressed out for years and wasn't able to be the type of mom she wanted to be at home.

Emma said before she started working with her CN boss that she was more social, more confident, and more of a go-getter. She felt relieved upon resigning her position and is starting to feel like her old self, but also finds herself questioning everyone, wondering whom she can trust. She is more suspicious of people now, and not as outgoing as she used to be.

This is a common result. Anyone who has been through years with a CN sees people and the world around them through different lenses. When in your experience "the nicest person in the world" turned out to be the most damaging, it is hard to trust anyone.

If any of these stories resonate with you, if you have been through something similar, know that you are not alone and it had nothing to do with you. You are smart and capable—there are people in this world who genuinely care about you.

My hope is that reading this chapter will validate your experience and your feelings and that the healing chapter will help carry you home, back to your beautiful self. You will get there, and you will be stronger than ever.

8

Sex with a Covert Narcissist

When Sara told me about her sex life with her CN husband of 25 years, I reassured her that it was a common story. I told her about so many other women I had talked to who shared similar experiences. She said, *"Please write about this in your book! I've never heard anyone say what you've just told me. I have felt so alone in this. I thought I was the only one. I thought something was wrong with me. I had come to the conclusion that I just wasn't a sexual person."*

Sex might be one of the most common methods of gaslighting a CN uses to control and manipulate. Most people don't notice. It's incredibly insidious. You can't get any more personal and vulnerable than your sex life. CNs use sex to manipulate through psychological means, making you feel as if something is wrong with you. When someone manipulates and controls you through sex, they set you up to think something is wrong with you so you blame yourself, you feel shame, and it affects your confidence and self-worth. You lose your ability to stand up for yourself because they are attacking the deepest parts of you. You end up isolating yourself because you don't want to admit to friends that after so many years of marriage, you haven't had an orgasm, that you feel no desire for sex, that your spouse/partner is completely disappointed in you, and that you feel like something is wrong with you sexually. You feel embarrassed. You shut down. It is incredibly personal. You believe whatever is wrong with your sex life is your fault, which is exactly what the CN wants you to think.

When you have sex with a CN, their pleasure is the most important thing; it is all about how they feel. You get the message you don't deserve pleasure and are subtly punished for having your own feelings, reactions, and confusion about what is happening in the bedroom. Your feelings don't matter to the CN.

Susan didn't have a sex drive for most of her marriage and couldn't figure out why. When she married her CN, she was young and a virgin. She had nothing for comparison. In her 25-year marriage, she never once had an orgasm. Feeling embarrassed and ashamed, she wondered what was wrong with her. Her husband seemed fine. He wanted sex, so she concluded *she* must be the problem.

This is not something she brought up to her friends. Most people don't. What woman in her forties wants to admit she has never had an orgasm with her partner? She was feeling enough despair; she didn't want to add to that by seeing people look at her with shock. She couldn't handle the thought of someone else judging her. She had enough of that from herself and her husband. So she stayed quiet about it for years. Over decades, she tried to "fix" herself, but when nothing helped, she wondered if she just wasn't a sexual person.

About a year after she divorced her CN, she went to a meditation retreat. A handsome, kind man showed her around the center. When he said hello and shook her hand, she felt sensations in her body she wasn't used to feeling. Something awakened inside her. Her eyes opened wide as the tingling feelings grew. Years later she married that man and now knows the truth—that she is a very sexual person who was manipulated, used, and made to believe she was not by her ex-CN. She is now healing from those years and being shown what real love actually looks and feels like.

Sex is one of the most powerful ways a CN controls their victim. When you have no desire for sex and can't figure out why, you feel bad that you are letting your partner down. They will let you know in various ways how much you are letting them down. They won't worry about you, what you are feeling and your struggles. That is not a concern to them because this relationship is not about you, or even the two of you—it is about the CN.

When Dawn dated her CN, the sex was great! They seemed to have an amazing connection. It was easy. He was romantic. He said all the right things that made her feel great about herself and her body. She felt pretty and sexy. They were very active sexually. This added to her believing he was the perfect match for her.

It is common for this to happen in the beginning. CNs mirror you sexually as well as emotionally during the love-bombing stage. They become you, act like you, so it feels as if you are in sync. You can't believe how good every part of this relationship is!

Soon after Dawn and her CN got married, things started to feel different. The love-bombing stage was over, and the subtle devaluing and demeaning stage began. She didn't notice anything different about the sex except how she felt. She told Brad, her CN husband, that she didn't know why, but every time they had sex she felt used. It didn't make any sense to her, but they were both open when it came to communication, so she wanted to let him know how she was feeling. He looked confused, acted like he cared, and seemed as though he wanted to hear.

Even though Brad's words were nice, Dawn could feel his anger toward her underneath them. The conversation began with her telling him how she felt used and somehow ended up with her apologizing and comforting *him*. He deflected the focus, didn't address her feelings, and instead turned the attention back on him as the "victim." She would continue to share with him how she felt over the years, but nothing ever changed. CNs aren't interested in looking at their own issues or changing any of their behaviors.

Dawn found herself unable to orgasm. Brad would show her articles in *Playboy* he had read about different positions he wanted to try, hoping it would help her orgasm. Even though it seemed like he was trying to help, she felt pressure to come through for him. He wanted her to orgasm so he would feel good about himself as a man and a lover. It never felt like he wanted her to experience pleasure for her, it was all about him feeling good about himself. Dawn's body knew she was not being loved and that she was not emotionally safe with Brad, so her body shut down. She lost all desire for sex.

Brad told Dawn how this affected him. He had needs, and she wasn't fulfilling them. She felt terrible. Even though this all started with her feeling used because her body, her intuition knew she was being used, it turned into her taking the blame for their diminishing sex life, feeling a heavy burden of shame and guilt, and believing something was wrong with her.

Dawn tried reading books and articles. She went to therapy. She tried all kinds of things to figure out what was wrong with her. At times, she wondered if her husband had a part in this, but she couldn't figure out how, so she took all the blame, and Brad did nothing to stop her from doing so.

Years went by; life kept going, they had kids, jobs, etc. They would address the sex issue here and there. Sex happened infrequently. She never enjoyed it and never climaxed. Brad used this to control Dawn for years. She felt like a terrible wife. Her husband became more and more distant. He punished her passive-aggressively for years, and she took it because she had started to believe she deserved it. When he was distant on dates together, irritable on every vacation, sabotaging every birthday, she felt like she shouldn't expect any better because she wasn't giving him much sex, so he didn't "owe her" his love and kindness.

Brad made comments over the years about how easy it would be for Dawn to be a nun, or wondering if she was a lesbian. As she gained weight over time, he made demeaning comments that kept her self-image low. She started to see herself as an overweight, non-sexual, hopeless disappointment.

Over the years, Brad brought up stories that made Dawn feel terrible and furthered her belief that everything really was her fault. Brad's stories became more dramatic during the discard phase. He would tell her how she damaged him from the beginning when she first saw his penis and didn't have a big reaction. She felt awful trying to recall that moment. It was so long ago. What did she do? What was her facial expression when she saw it? She got the message she had completely crushed his manhood. Even as she told me her story, she still couldn't see the manipulation and felt horrible that she had wounded him so deeply.

This is what CNs do. They rely on your pity. They rely on your tender heart. They manipulate you into believing you are terrible.

When this happens, they have you in the palm of their hand and can control you for years. It was all about Brad. He wanted Dawn to prove his manhood to him. He did not care about how she felt. He did not want her to feel pleasure because he loved her so much and delighted in her feeling good. She never felt loved by him in bed because the truth was that she wasn't. She never felt cherished because she wasn't.

She had never shared this story with anyone before she told me because she felt such shame. The reality is that even if Dawn had reached orgasm, her CN husband would have found something else "wrong" with her.

That is what happened to Melanie. Her story was a lot like Dawn's except toward the end of her longtime marriage, she had a sexual awakening after going on a trip with her girlfriends and working up the courage to confide in them about the fact she had never had an orgasm with her husband. When she got home, she started to explore herself and was able to bring herself to orgasm. She was so excited to try with her CN husband after years of feeling like a giant disappointment to him sexually and when she did, she was finally able to orgasm.

Suddenly she wanted sex all the time. She would jump on him every day. She was so excited to orgasm with him and finally give him what he had been wanting for so many years. After about a week of sex every day, he told her he didn't want to have sex with her anymore because now all she wanted to do was orgasm and he didn't feel like she really cared about him.

When you are with a CN, you can never win no matter what you do. They will never be fully satisfied with you. You will never be good enough in their eyes. They have to have something they can hold over you in order to control and manipulate you.

The biggest area in which Melanie's husband could control her was now gone. He couldn't blame her for not wanting sex. He couldn't use that as an excuse to put her down and treat her badly. After becoming stronger inside and now sexual, she could no longer be his supply, so after 18 years of marriage, he was done. He moved out and a few months later moved on to another target.

When you live with someone who slowly brainwashes you to think you are the problem or that certain things are wrong with you, it takes time and a lot of undoing to be able to see clearly again. Dawn, for instance, is getting stronger and beginning to see through the manipulation and control she experienced for so many years.

Often what we don't notice with these relationships is what doesn't happen, what isn't there. Dawn's husband never went to counseling to see if there was something in him that might be causing her to feel used. He didn't ever feel bad that she felt bad. He never felt empathy. She felt terrible about letting him down. She had imagined for years what it might be like to be in his shoes because she had empathy. He never once felt terrible for letting her down, for the fact she was not experiencing great sex. He didn't care. He never looked into ways he could make her feel more safe and loved. He did not pursue her because he loved her and wanted their relationship to be strong. He let her feel responsible and badly about herself. He was okay with her feeling down and confused. He was okay with hurting her with his words. She did not matter to him. He did not love her. He projected his own sexual issues onto her and had allowed her to take the blame.

Sex is always confusing when you are with a covert narcissist— you never ever feel good enough. I've talked to both men and women, and it is the same story every time. Not having orgasms is also a common theme with survivors. When your body doesn't feel safe with someone, it can't relax and have its natural release. Your body knows way before your mind figures things out.

CNs twist things when it comes to sex. One woman I spoke with said toward the end of her 15-year relationship, her CN husband became obsessed with the idea of Brazilian waxes. He told her lots of women in porn videos have everything waxed. He wanted her to do that to her body. He told her he would like it better if she did. When she shared with him that she felt uncomfortable with the idea, he pushed more and told her he was deeply hurt by the fact she didn't want to do this for him. He told her that by not getting waxed she was showing him she didn't care about him because she knew how much this would mean to him. It didn't matter that it made her uncomfortable. Only his own feelings mattered to him.

When the average person hears this story, it's easy to think, *What a jerk! Why would anyone stay with someone like that?* Like most victims, this woman is lovely. She is smart, super smart in fact. But when you have lived through such love bombing and years of intermittent reinforcement, these conversations mess with your mind and heart because you believe this person loves and cares about you. It is easy for them to manipulate you into thinking you are being selfish and inconsiderate. The CN was projecting his own selfishness onto her, making her wonder if she was being selfish. He was emotionally immature, but she didn't see that because she had also experienced years of kindness and tenderness from this man.

CNs know your vulnerabilities. They know what will affect you and reinforce your insecurities and self-doubt. They know how to exploit your empathy and caring heart, to use it against you and control you.

As a life coach, I see patterns and metaphors when people talk to me about things they are struggling with. I notice when pieces fit together to form a picture as I listen to clients share their stories.

As I heard more men and women disclose intimate details of their sex life with their CN, a pattern began to emerge in my mind.

The discard phase is excruciating. It is also extremely confounding, to say the least. You saw your CN as one person for years, and now you see someone you don't recognize, someone cruel and unfeeling. Your head is spinning, and your heart is devastated. You've never experienced betrayal, hurt, and confusion like this before. Victims look back over the years trying to figure out what happened. Once someone brings up the idea that their partner might be a narcissist, they search again for signs they missed, traits they didn't notice.

Here are common thoughts victims have when trying to figure things out:

> *What was the truth of the relationship? Is this person I lived with and loved really who they said they were? Was I manipulated? Narcissism is such a strong word.*
>
> *Was I really the cause of this not working out? Am I really as awful as they are saying I am? Did they ever really love me?*
>
> *Was it all an act? Is that even possible? Am I over-dramatizing this narcissist diagnosis?*
>
> *Are they really innocent and I just can't move on for some reason? Was I difficult to live with and just don't see it?*

A victim's mind goes crazy with so many thoughts and analyzations. Trying to see clearly can feel impossible or futile. There is a way to discover the truth of the relationship, and the secret decoder, I began to realize, is sex. This is the pattern I saw as I interviewed people. I tested my theory with many survivors and each time, the process I'm about to explain blew them away. It opened their eyes to the truth and helped them finally see through the smoke and mirrors.

It is so easy to believe the CN is telling the truth because they act so confidently. They can sound so reasonable, and you are used to trusting them. The thing is, they are professional liars. Your body, on the other hand, is an accurate barometer that will always tell you the truth. You can trust it more than anything and anyone. How you felt during and after sex is the blueprint for the truth of your relationship. Here is how this works…

Answer the following questions, then I will explain.

1. Describe sex at the beginning of your relationship. What was your partner like? How did they treat you in bed? How did you feel when you had sex with them? Be as detailed as you can. For instance, it's common for victims to say it was great. Find more descriptions. Maybe he was tender? Attentive? Did she say flattering things about your body? Maybe it was fun? Adventurous? Easy? Great connection?

_____

_____

_____

_____

_____

_____

Your answers to the first question describe what the love-bombing phase was like for you and your partner. This describes how the CN portrayed him or herself and what you have believed about this person for years.

2. When did sex start to feel different? What was the difference? How did you feel during sex? After? What were they like? How did they treat you? How did you feel about sex with them? How did you feel about yourself, sexually? Describe the evolution of your sexual relationship. The more detailed you are, the more helpful this will be for you.

_____

_____

_____

_____

_____

_____

_____

_____

_____

_____

_____

_____

What you have just described is the truth of the entire relationship and the truth of who your partner really is.

I'm going to show you one woman's answers and then explain how they reveal the truth of the relationship with her CN to help you see how this works. It will help as you reflect on your own experience. I have heard many similar responses from other men and women:

> *"It felt confusing. I felt frustrated. I felt like he was normal and there was something wrong with me since I didn't desire sex and he did. He was passive. He put it all on me to initiate and acted like a martyr when I didn't want to. He felt disconnected. He was not in tune with me. I had to tell him what to do. It didn't feel like making love, more like an act. It didn't feel like he was making love to me, or in love with me. He was not passionate. He felt robotic. It felt one-sided. I felt like I was being used. It was all about him. He wasn't tender. He blamed me for us not having a good sex life. He took no responsibility even though he said he did. He would sometimes say nice compliments about my body. It never felt like I could connect with him on a deep level. He looked out for himself sexually and didn't ever look out for me. He had sexual issues from his childhood but made me feel like I was the one with sexual issues. I believed I was the cause of our unfulfilling sex life. I felt like an object. It felt like it was on his terms and he would get mad when I didn't go along with what he wanted. He would then punish me with the silent treatment and demeaning comments. It wasn't fun. It felt like it was all up to me to make it work. I felt like I was just there to make him feel good about himself. It didn't feel authentic from*

> *him. It almost felt like he was playing a role. His body felt limp, like there was no life in him."*

Now I will take the above description and use it to describe the relationship as a whole. The portion in italics is how she described her sex life with the CN. The regular print is what the statement reveals about the relationship and about the CN:

It felt confusing. The relationship was confusing. *It felt frustrating.* She felt frustrated in the relationship. *I felt like he was normal and there was something wrong with me since I didn't desire sex and he did.* He manipulated her into thinking he was normal, and something was wrong with her. Her feelings didn't matter. *He was passive.* He was passive in the relationship. *He put it all on me to initiate and acted like a martyr when I didn't want to.* He used the role of being a victim to control her. He played on her guilt and shame. He took no personal responsibility and put it all on her to make the relationship work. He manipulated her through pouting so she would feel sorry for him, thinking she was causing his unhappiness. *He felt disconnected.* He was disconnected from himself and because of that was unable to connect with anyone else. *He was not in tune with me.* He was not in tune with her in the relationship, nor did he have a desire to be, as demonstrated by his actions. *I had to tell him what to do.* He acted like a baby. She had to spoon-feed him, explaining basic concepts to a grown man. *It didn't feel like making love, more like an act.* There was no real love in the marriage from him. It was all an act. *It didn't feel like he was making love to me, or was in love with me.* He didn't actually love her. *He was not passionate.* There was no passion from him in the relationship. *He felt robotic.* Any life in the relationship was from her. He was hollow inside. *It felt one-sided.* He wanted her to supply him with life and an identity because he did not have a strong sense of who he was. The relationship was one-sided. It was up to her to bring life to it, or there would be none. *I felt like I was being used.* She was being used in the relationship. It was all about him. The relationship was all about him. *He wasn't tender.* He wasn't tender to her in the relationship. *He blamed me for us not having a good sex life.* He blamed her for things that were not her fault. He was emotionally immature, weak, and selfish. *He took no responsibility even though he said he did.* He took no responsibility in the relationship even though he said he did. His actions did not match his words. *He would sometimes say nice compliments about my body.* He gave her intermittent reinforcement. She experienced years of a mixture of subtle cruelty and niceties. *It never felt like I could connect with him on a deep level.* No matter what she did, there was no way she could have connected with him on a deep level. A deep authentic connection with him was not possible. *He looked out for himself sexually and didn't ever look out for me.* He looked out for himself; he did not look out for her in the relationship. *He had sexual issues from his childhood but made me feel like I was the one with sexual issues.* He had unresolved issues from his childhood, but instead of being honest about that, he projected his issues onto her. *I believed I was the cause of our unfulfilling sex life.* He blamed her for the relationship not working and she accepted the blame. *I felt like an object.* She was an object that was easily replaceable to him. *It felt like it was on his terms and he would get mad when I didn't go along with what he wanted.* He was controlling and manipulative by forcing things to be on his terms and getting mad when she didn't go along with what he wanted. He had the maturity level of a toddler, wanting his way and throwing a tantrum when he didn't get it. *He would then punish me with the silent treatment and demeaning comments.* He would punish her with the silent treatment and demeaning comments in the relationship. *It wasn't fun.* The relationship wasn't fun, to say the least. *It felt like it was all up to me to make it work.* He put the full responsibility on her to make the relationship work. *I felt like I was just there to make him feel good about himself.* He only wanted her there to make him feel good about himself. *It didn't feel authentic from him.* He wasn't authentic. *It almost felt like he was playing a role.* He was playing a role. He was acting. *His body felt limp, like there was no life in him.* He was a shell of a man who felt limp to her in bed because that was the truth of his spirit. He relied on her for life.

In my research, I also asked this question of friends who are in healthy, loving relationships to see the contrast and test my theory further. These are honest people who don't sugarcoat things. Before I asked, I thought, *I'm sure they have some issues in their sex life. Doesn't everyone?* I was amazed by their answers.

- *"Sex is fun with my husband."*
- *"I feel loved, safe."*
- *"I feel beautiful."*
- *"I feel sexy when I'm with him."*
- *"He is very gentle and attentive."*
- *"He loves to give me pleasure and see me feeling really good."*
- *"It feels playful."*
- *"I feel incredibly loved and cherished by him."*
- *"He is very sensitive and kind."*
- *"Even when it's mediocre, it's still good. During those times we just laugh."*
- *"I feel very connected and cherished."*
- *"We feel in sync."*
- *"It feels like we are dancing."*

These are all people who have been married more than 17 years. Some more than 20. Their lives have not been easy. These are not young couples who are starting fresh. Relationships are hard work, but these people are not married to narcissists, and their sex life reflects the truth of what they feel as well as experience in their marriage.

Sex is a reflection of the truth of your relationship. It also demonstrates you can trust yourself. If you were in a relationship where you lost the desire for sex, it was because your body is smart. It knew you were not emotionally safe with your partner. If you experienced real love, you would have wanted sex, you would have reached orgasms, and it would have felt like love every time. You would have felt protected, respected, and cherished.

Recently, I came across a picture of what looked like a vagina but was, in fact, an image of vocal cords. It struck me how powerful this was when I thought these are the two areas in which we are controlled and suppressed by CNs the most. Our voice—the freedom we have to express our worries, feelings, and desires—are silenced as a way of controlling us. Our expression of love and passion is suppressed by the one who is supposed to love us the most.

Sex is one of the most vulnerable activities in life. CNs take this sacred act and use it against us, to quiet us, to quell our spirits and drain the life from us. Our sexual selves bring life to this earth, and CNs use it to suppress the lifeforce within us. It is cruel and inhumane. In ancient cultures, when shamans (spiritual and ceremonial leaders and healers among indigenous civilizations) meet people looking for healing, one of the first questions they ask is, *"When did you stop singing?"* Most targets told me they had so much life in them before their relationship with a CN. Through years of disguised abuse, that life, that light within them, slowly diminished without notice. They accepted this as who they were, unaware the singing had stopped, forgetting the dancers they used to be.

Sex with a CN is a form of emotional assault; it is psychological abuse, concealed abuse that shuts you down inside. You are left feeling "less than," unwanted, undesirable, and unworthy of love. You lose the truth of who you are. You were used and discarded, and it was not your fault.

It was never your fault.

The fact that this happened to you is not a small thing. You have suffered a trauma with no visible scars, but your body, your spirit feels it. It is important to allow yourself to recognize and feel the gravity of what you have been through. Your heart, your internal landscape, has taken a beating, and now it needs time to heal and to restore.

What you feel is valid and important. Be kind to yourself. You deserve love and gentleness. Be that for yourself.

The more you take care of yourself and treat yourself with exquisite kindness, the more your body will get used to that feeling and cease to tolerate anything less from anyone else. You will grow stronger every day, and one day you will have the real thing, all of it. You deserve someone to love who loves to give you pleasure. They will love to see you feeling great because they love you. They will genuinely care about you, and you will feel the amazing difference. This time, making love will actually feel like making *love*.

9

Divorcing a Covert Narcissist

An amicable divorce is not possible when you are dealing with a covert narcissist. The breakup is sudden. It is a fire hose of so many different traits. You will experience intermittent reinforcement, smear campaigns, flying monkeys, lies, manipulation, crazy-making conversations, triangulation, absolute absence of empathy, devaluing and demeaning insults, emotional immaturity, profound selfishness, entitled superiority, and so much more during this discard phase. You will feel a betrayal like you've never known.

The "nice guy/gal" you were convinced you loved and who loved you back becomes someone you do not recognize and would never tolerate if you were to meet them today. Experiencing this throws you into a tailspin. The chaos and cruelty you experience from this person you loved with all your heart are unfathomable. The constant criticism, both cloaked and blatant, causes you to feel paralyzed. You find it hard to build a new life. The discard phase is both physically and emotionally debilitating.

The Breakup

Many people told me their breakups happened when they were out of town, so they didn't have the comfort and security of home. They were out of their element and felt more vulnerable, unprotected, and alone. This is not a coincidence. The CN creates experiences to get you rattled, defenseless, and out of sorts. The discard will feel sudden, but the reality is the CN has been planning it for a long time without you knowing.

Leading up to "the talk" will feel like a bewildering time. Their behavior will not be what you are used to seeing. CNs often will make new friends who they will confide in about how terrible you are and how they can't take it anymore. They will tell their new friend stories about you that will make this person feel so badly for them and encourage them to end the relationship with you. The new friends will support the CN and help them in any way they can. CNs will make sure and let you know their friend agrees with them. For a time, they become part of the CN's flying monkeys crew until the CN moves on when their new friend no longer serves a purpose.

"Not many men would have lasted this long being married to you!" Sarah's CN husband told her during his breakup speech. This statement is just one example of CNs being incredibly cruel with the words they hurl at you. You will feel paralyzed and numb. You will feel trauma reverberating its way through your precious body. They will seem soulless. You will be devastated, but they will seem like they are just crossing something off their to-do list. They appear eerily unfazed by the relationship ending. You are falling apart while they seem completely fine. You feel like you are in the twilight zone, and they are happily making plans to move out.

Early one morning, before they were to go on a family vacation, Emily couldn't sleep. She walked down to the kitchen to make some coffee and saw her CN husband's phone lying on the counter. Something told her to look at his text messages. She had never been one to spy on him, but with his recent strange behavior, she decided to take a look. She found a conversation from the day before where he and his new friend were talking about how excited they were for him to move in after his family vacation. They both went on and on saying how much they were looking forward to this and couldn't wait to live together and do all the fun things they had planned.

Emily had been crying daily, their kids had been confused and devastated wondering what was going on, but the CN husband was over-the-moon excited for his new adventure; he hadn't mentioned anything to Emily or their kids.

When your relationship appears to be ending, your world is falling apart; you are devastated. Your CN is unaffected. It makes you feel like you're going crazy. To give perspective, this often happens to victims after 20 years of marriage. Some I talked to experienced this after 30, even 40 years of marriage.

It is common for the CN to initiate the breakup, but for the victim to be the one to file for divorce. The CN will make it very clear they are done but won't take any action to end the marriage because their reputation is their number-one priority and they don't want to look like the bad guy/gal. Some CNs drag this out for years. It takes a lot of courage for the survivors to file for divorce because they are made to feel so guilty and shameful by the CN and their flying monkeys. The victims are painted as the ones who didn't try and who ended the relationship, singlehandedly breaking up a family.

Sudden and Complete Abandonment

It is very common for a CN to leave their spouse with all or most of the responsibilities of life. I talked to many women who were left to sell the home, figure out the school situation for the kids, move everything, sell furniture, tie up loose ends, take care of the kids, sort out the bills, etc. The CN moves on quickly and completely abandons you to clean up the wreckage.

You may have been with this person for decades, and suddenly they are gone. You are left to pick up the pieces, to make big decisions while you are an emotional mess.

The Contrast

For a victim, the fact the relationship is ending comes as a shock and they are devastated. On the other hand, the CN is eerily untouched by emotion.

You are falling apart, and they are moving on, letting you know how much happier they are. You are hurt and confused, and they are acting like it is not that big of a deal. You are still yourself, and they are behaving like someone you have never seen before. The way they treat you leaves you stunned, shocked, and mystified.

You are trying to understand and connect with them while they are putting you down. They have no interest in connecting with you or working to heal the relationship. They put no effort into making it work after so many years of building a life together. When they are done, they are done.

They have no empathy, no concern for your feelings, no guilt, and no semblance of a conscience. It is all about them. It always has been, it is just more obvious now. They will appear cold and unfeeling, and you are left wondering what in the world is happening.

The New Target

CNs move on quickly to a new target, in many cases before the divorce. They will be with this person, but not tell their friends. It is important for them to look good and for their flying monkeys to still believe in them as the victim and feel sorry for them.

The new target is thrilled and feels so lucky to have found such a great person, just like you felt in the beginning. The CN will tell all kinds of stories about you, painting a picture to the new target of how awful you are. The new target feels sorry for the CN and becomes their new devotee.

There is no sensitivity or empathy with CNs, so while you are falling apart, they will make sure their new life with their new supply looks amazing. They will let you know how happy they are now that they are finally rid of you and with someone so much better.

During the end of the relationship, you might wonder if they are with someone else. You will bring it up to them and instead of being honest they will either not answer you or divert your attention elsewhere and bring up all the things that are wrong with you. You are too sensitive, you need to move on, you are a jealous person, paranoid, etc. They will say things to keep you unglued and looking like a mess while they calmly ride into the sunset with their new target.

Most of the time, CNs move to targets who are empathetic and nurturing, but sometimes they choose another narcissist. If they do this it means both narcissists want something from the other, and when they aren't getting that anymore, the relationship will end.

Not only do you receive an influx of emotional abuse during this time, but on top of that, you have to watch them portray their new perfect life in front of you. Know this: things are never as they appear with CNs. It is not perfect. The CN is not truly happy and never will be. These people are filled with silent rage and no empathy. With that combination, only manufactured happiness is possible, but never deep, authentic happiness. It is just a show to rattle you. You will get stronger and clearer, and someday this show they are portraying won't affect you anymore.

Smear Campaign

CNs are very strategic in how they manipulate people. They will tell stories in a way that keeps them looking like a genuine person who really cares and is just trying to do the right thing. Their flying monkeys will hear their distorted view of reality and see you as the horrible enemy who is causing all the pain. For instance, when Amy was going through her divorce she received a scathing email from her CN's sister telling her this divorce was all her fault.

These messages are incredibly difficult to receive, and they are common. No matter how you respond, these people are blinded to the truth of the CN just like you were for years.

The CN's smear campaign doesn't end after the divorce. This can go on for years. They don't want you to be happy. They don't want to see you doing well. This is another thing that sets this divorce apart from normal divorces. They still want to control you and your life and the stronger you get, the more you don't engage in their nonsense, they try to find other ways to hurt you.

Four years after her divorce, Amy's mom received an email out of the blue from Amy's CN ex-husband. In the email, he said how concerned he was. He told Amy's mom how much he loved and respected her and had always appreciated how kind she had been to him. He told her how hard it was for him to write this email, but that he needed to tell her the "truth" about her daughter. The CN wrote tales of how Amy had been using her mom for her money, how she had been hoarding money from their kids and lying to her mom all these years. It was an extensive email depicting himself as a person who really cared and Amy as someone her own mom should not trust. Amy told me her CN ex had not spoken to her mom for more than four years. He clearly did not care about her. This was his manipulative way of trying to get to Amy. She was becoming stronger, establishing firmer boundaries. Because of this, she was not as easily manipulated. He tried to hurt her by attempting to sever relationships with people who love her. He was losing control of her. This was one attempt to keep that control.

Normal people move on whereas CNs don't.

This can be incredibly confusing for family members and friends of victims who have also experienced the CN as a kind and loving individual. They have also been lied to and manipulated by the CN in your life. CNs affect many people. If they are an ex-spouse, the ripple effects are seemingly endless: they affect you, your parents, your siblings, and your close friends. If they are a parent, they also affect your children.

Money

CNs want you to feel unhinged, vulnerable, and scared. They will often use money as a way to control you. Normal people in a divorce situation typically try to be fair. CNs will try to give you the least amount of money possible and extract it from you as soon as they possibly can. I've seen this across the board. It is one of the biggest ways they try to control you and punish you. Many women I talked to were stay-at-home moms or women who earned a small income, and their CN husband was the main breadwinner in the family. Because of this imbalance, their survival was dependent on the financial support they got from their CN.

CNs know their victim is dependent on them for money and use that ammunition every chance they get.

They will do things such as transfer all the money into another bank account so you can't get to it. This makes you afraid, and it is when you are most vulnerable to their control and manipulation. They have you as their prisoner. You cannot survive without them. Usually, you are the one who is taking responsibility for the kids. The way CNs treat women and men who have loved them, been good to them for years, often decades is deplorable. The women and men I met are such quality people, and absolutely none of them deserved the treatment they received.

CNs will use whatever means possible to keep from giving you the money you deserve. They will use intimidation, bullying tactics, and play on your sympathetic heart.

It was so difficult for Joanne to believe her husband of over 25 years was manipulating her and had been for so many years. She had just discovered he might be a CN and had started researching the subject of narcissism. The night before mediation where they would decide how much support she would get from her husband, he sent her an email. He asked her to please think about his health (he was in good health). He said he didn't like the idea of supporting her for a long time. It was causing him a lot of stress; he pleaded, *"Please think of me when we are in mediation."*

She felt so much anxiety after reading it. She didn't know what to do, what to think. Without support, she would be homeless. After years of being a stay-at-home mom and having no assets, his salary was all she had. She would be starting from scratch after raising kids and having minimum-wage jobs for years. She had worked some part-time jobs here and there, but she knew she would need time to build something to be able to support herself. She was panicked, but also didn't want to make things hard for him. She still loved him and thought of him as a good person who cared about her, too.

Joanne forwarded the email to her attorney and asked her advice as to how to respond. Her attorney wrote back with one word: *"Whatever."*

When she saw her attorney at the beginning of mediation, Joanne asked, *"What did you mean when you said 'whatever'?"*

"His email was so manipulative," the attorney responded.

"Really? Please show me how because I don't see it."

Her attorney pulled up the email and started pointing out things Joanne hadn't noticed. *"Every paragraph is the same pattern. Look. First, he compliments you, then he puts you down, and then he ends with a pity statement. Next paragraph. First, he compliments you, then he puts you down, then he ends with a pity statement. Last paragraph. First, he compliments you, then he puts you down, then he ends with a pity statement. Next paragraph..."*

Joanne couldn't believe it. When she looked at it again she was stunned. Frozen. Now questioning everything. *Was this conscious? How could it not be? What else hadn't she seen?*

If he had just been cruel, she would not have been affected like she was, but the nastiness was mixed with kindness and feigned vulnerability that played on her tender heart. This threw her into a place in her mind where she couldn't think straight or see clearly. She still believed he was the guy she first fell in love with.

Victims need really good attorneys. The tough thing is that because a lot of the CNs hold all the power and control of the money, many survivors cannot afford a good attorney. If you can afford an attorney, find one who is educated on narcissism. You need someone who understands and will not be bullied or allow you to be bullied. If you don't have the funds, there are many helpful non-profit groups that can assist with legal issues and advice. A woman I spoke with saved thousands of dollars working with a local group in her area. I would also recommend joining a support group and asking others for advice with financial issues. Many of them have been through what you are going through and will have valuable information and insights for you.

Attorneys/Mediators/Judges

I am not an attorney and cannot give you legal advice. I can tell you things others have told me that helped them through the legal process of divorcing a covert narcissist.

Know that the CN will charm their own attorney, the mediator, and the judge if you have to go to court. They will come across as a goodhearted person who really cares about their kids and is just trying to abide by the law. This is why you need a good attorney or a strong friend who sees right through the CN's acting abilities to come with you to mediation.

It helps to have someone supporting you who is thinking clearly because this is a highly emotional and unnerving time for you. Your world is crashing around you, the one you love is treating you like garbage, and you are filled with fear about how you are going to support yourself and your kids.

The CN will trigger you during mediations or other meetings. They know the things to say that will throw you off and rattle you so you won't be able to think clearly. They will say things or have the mediator say things to you that they know will cause you to come unglued. They want you to look like the crazy one. They want to come across as the calm, stable one, so the judge or mediator will allow things to go their way. Make sure your mediation is set up in such a way that you never see the CN because of how it might affect you. The mediator can walk back and forth between your room and theirs.

Even after things have been settled financially, it's likely they will still come after you over the years until the support time is over. For instance, the state where Charlene lives required her CN ex to pay her child support until their son turned 19. He graduated high school early and started college when he was 17. The CN came after Charlene to legally take child support away from her because he decided she didn't need it anymore since their son didn't live with her. She was paying for all his college expenses including his tuition. She had also bought him a car. She was paying all his bills, and he came home to visit her on weekends and holidays.

The CN successfully took back all child support from Charlene for their son. He refused to pay anything to help him with college and told his son that Charlene was a manipulative, controlling, materialistic mom who only wanted money. A few months later, the son left college and moved back in with Charlene. She continued to take care of him, pay his student loan payments, pay for groceries, and pay all the bills in the home with no child support. That is what survivors do. They are kindhearted people who take care of their kids no matter what. They are the opposite of CNs.

The legal process is daunting, scary, and overwhelming. Make sure you find support. You will need it. You will also grow from this experience and see a strength come out of you that you may not have known you had. It is hard to accept that the person you married is not who they appeared to be and the way they are treating you really is who they are. The more you can see this, though, the less you will get triggered and the easier it will be to make decisions for yourself and your kids.

You will get through this. Time will pass. You will educate yourself, get support, and become incredibly strong. Breathe deeply and take excellent care of yourself during this time.

Using the Kids

CNs will use your kids against you because they use whatever they know will hurt and affect you the most. They do not care how this affects their kids.

Some CNs will talk to their kids in a way that is very subtle, planting seeds of doubt about the other parent. The older the kids are, the more covert the manipulation will be. Triangulation can also come into play where the CN pits the children and the other parent against each other, and none of them notice who the instigator is. CNs use kids as pawns. It is incredibly sad. Children are also supplies for the CNs, and they will align with the child who gives them no conflict, but still thinks they are a good, innocent person.

With legal authorities and to their flying monkeys, CNs will talk as if they really care about their kids, but their actions never match their words. However, they are so convincing and seem so sincere that judges, mediators, and attorneys tend to believe the pictures they paint.

CNs will use matters that involve kids to make your life difficult. Mary's CN husband insisted their daughter go to a certain school. He hired an attorney, ordered Mary to meet an arbitrator, and convinced the attorney and arbitrator to make Mary pull their daughter out of school and put her in another one. He had done no research. He knew nothing about the school. He didn't care about their daughter. This was just one way he could control Mary and cause her to experience as much stress as possible. Mary, on the other hand, had spent hours studying schools in the area, stopping by to visit and setting up meetings with principals and teachers. She actually cared about their daughter and wanted the best for her. Her ex-husband bullied her and convinced the arbitrator he was a loving husband trying to do the right thing, dealing with a crazy ex-wife.

These divorces can be shocking and confusing for kids. Usually, when you have a marriage with a CN, there isn't a lot of fighting. It looks pretty perfect to everyone, including the kids. It is common for them to think their parents were fine and be completely blindsided by the divorce, just like their survivor parent. Older kids can view the marriage as just not working out, not a good match. The CN will sometimes foster this idea to minimize their abusive behavior. Painting a picture that they just weren't a good match devalues and minimizes trauma the victim has experienced and is experiencing and makes them question them self once again.

The Rules are Different

Well-meaning people will give you advice that helped them in their divorce. The thing to keep in mind is, if they did not divorce a covert narcissist, the "rules" of the dissolution are different. It's a whole other world. They mean well and are trying to help but have no idea how much they don't (and can't) understand.

"Make sure you and your ex communicate a lot. It's healthier for the kids." If you have a healthy ex, this is true. If you have a CN ex, this does not work and is a terrible idea. CNs are not interested in resolving issues or finding harmonious solutions to conflicts that arise. They use conversations to confuse, control, and manipulate you. They will attempt to throw you off-kilter and keep you wobbling. They want you to not be able to see and think clearly. If you have kids together, keep the communication as limited as possible with the CN and stick to the facts. Stay away from emotional and personal conversations. Coordinate plans and leave it at that.

They will try to rope you into talking about personal things. They will try to trigger you through emails and texts. Take time before you respond. Breathe. Write back calmly, ignoring anything personal they said. Stick to logistics that need to be discussed. Keep your responses simple and to the point. Trying to engage in personal conversations with them is futile and will just bring you more pain. They want you to lose it. They want you to be unsteady, that way they can control you more. Stand firm and guard yourself. They don't deserve to see your precious heart. And you deserve to be with people who love and protect your heart. Call a trusted friend to help you see clearly and remind you what love looks like.

"Make sure you never talk bad about your ex to your kids." Part of this is true; you should not turn to your kids to vent or seek support. They are not your friends; they are not your counselors; they are your kids. Make sure you don't just spout off about their CN dad or mom when you feel angry. This takes a lot of self-control, but it is worth it to hold your tongue. Call a friend to vent.

There are, however, times it is helpful for kids to hear from you that certain behavior is not okay. If their CN dad or mom speaks badly about you to them, they need to know that's not acceptable. If the CN parent said something that is affecting the child's self-worth, that's not okay; you can counter the wrong information by letting them know how worthy of respect they are. You can explain to them what love is supposed to look like so they can grow up recognizing unhealthy behavior and choose love instead. This will help them be healthy people and choose partners who will truly love them.

With most separations, there are hurt feelings and there is anger, though usually after time, things calm down. Not so with a CN. Even years after the divorce is finalized, they will still smear your name and try to control and manipulate you and put you down. This happens particularly if you are the one who filed for divorce. That creates something called a "narcissistic injury," which a CN rarely gets over. Any threat to their ego causes this. The constant revenge is startling. This is who they are; it has nothing to do with you. The best thing you can do is heal and learn the truth so you can see through their façade. The stronger you get, the less they will affect you.

Crazy-Making Conversations

During the discard phase, conversations with a CN are strange, disorienting, and even ridiculous. In *Psychopath Free*, author Jackson MacKenzie calls these conversations "word salad."

> *"The psychopath (psychopaths and narcissists have similar traits) will often use word salad in an attempt to keep your mind occupied. Basically, it's a conversation from hell. They aren't actually saying anything at all; they are just talking to you. Before you can even respond to one outrageous statement, they're already on to the next. You'll be left with your head spinning."*

The things they say to you are a mix of partial truths, blatant lies, weird conclusions, strange thinking, hurls of insults, compliments, "poor me" proclamations, and superior thinking. They speak to you in an exceedingly condescending way.

Depression

CNs are relentless with their abuse. They will kick you when you are down without any remorse or apparent conscience. They treat you as if you deserve nothing, as if you are trash on the street. This damages your self-image and self-worth. Going through a divorce with a CN can tear you down emotionally. Denise bravely shared a recent journal entry with me that she wrote during her divorce proceedings: *"I don't want to be here anymore. There is nothing more for me here. It doesn't feel like there is anything left for me here. I think the kids will be okay if I took my life. They would be sad for a bit, but then they would be okay. I just can't do this anymore. It's too much pain."*

144

Victims such as Denise experience very low times where they cannot think straight. The barrage of verbal and emotional abuse takes its toll. Dealing with a CN can make you lose the will to live. Denise did make it through her divorce. She knows now her kids would not have been okay. She is extremely glad she did not take action and is now working on rebuilding her life.

If you are feeling this sense of despair, I want you to know you are not alone. Take one day at a time. Keep getting up every morning. Call a friend. Go to a support group. Spend time in nature. Be extraordinarily kind to yourself. This will pass. You will get through this, and you will come out the other side with more strength, love, and compassion than you ever imagined.

You are experiencing the effects of narcissistic abuse. This is not your fault. Do not believe a word your CN says. None of it comes from a place of love. And that is exactly what you need right now—lots and lots of love. Surround yourself with people who sincerely know you and love you. Listen to them, not your abuser.

Congratulations

If you were the one to file for divorce, you might be feeling shame over that, wondering if you did the right thing. I want you to know that what you did took a tremendous amount of courage and strength. You stopped taking the abuse. You stood up for yourself. You made a choice to respect yourself, and you set a strong example for your children and those around you. Abuse in all forms is wrong and must not be tolerated anymore by any of us. You took a stand that not everyone does. What you did requires emotional fortitude, resiliency, and grit.

By filing the paperwork, you said *no more*. No more devaluing, no more demeaning, no more health issues, no more sexual confusion, no more psychological torment. No more lies, controlling, insults, and disrespect. You stood up for love. You made the choice to protect your heart, your mind, and your body. By doing what you did, you gave others courage without realizing it.

You are incredibly strong! I bow to you in honor and respect of who you are and what you've done.

10

Why Do They Emotionally and Psychologically Abuse?

I've been to many support-group meetings, listened to podcasts and videos, and read articles and books where people have shared the reasons they think covert narcissists psychologically and emotionally abuse people. Some of those theories include: they harm others because they were abused as a child; they hate themselves; their childhood needs were not met; they do not see people as people; they love themselves too much; they like to feel superior; they are reacting to feeling unseen, misunderstood, or traumatized as a child; they weren't loved growing up; they were spoiled and idealized as a child; they were raised with mixed messages of grandiosity and worthlessness.

Here is the conclusion I have personally formulated: we don't really know for sure why they abuse, and it doesn't really matter.

I say this because I care about you and I've seen how victims can spend so much time and energy trying to figure out the CN in their life that they get stuck in the mire of the darkness of narcissism and never give their own light a chance to come forth.

Many of the reasons listed in that first paragraph may be true, and yes, it is good as a society to learn the psychology behind why people do the things they do, and there are times it helps to understand. If that helps you and you find you are able to heal and separate from the CN, then do that. Your body knows what works best for you and what you need to heal and get strong. But if you find yourself feeling exhausted trying to figure out why the CN in your life treats you the way they do, then it might be time to let that part of your journey go as you focus on healing and strengthening yourself.

Victims are such caring people that it is easy for us to spend our lives focused on others. This is a beautiful thing if we are helping others who really want our help and making sure we are taking care of ourselves at the same time. One man I talked to who was married for 25 years to a CN still feels sorry for his ex-wife, believing she treats him badly because she is wounded and needs love. He is such a special and smart man with a tender heart and is having a hard time breaking free from her.

I am a very caring person myself, and I also see people as wounded. Most of us are. I am interested in learning why we do the things we do, but I have noticed a trend of victims immersing themselves in this mission to figure out why. It leads to diversions, never healing themselves, and paralyzes them from moving on. It is easy for us to get caught up in the idea of an abuser being wounded, being a victim themselves, and not hold them accountable for their actions. Remember, they do have free will. They have choices just like we do. They are not helpless. They can help their behavior.

We made excuses for our CN's abusive behavior for years. Some of them sounded like:

- *"He had a rough childhood."*
- *"She doesn't know how to love because she didn't have a good mom."*
- *"He had an abusive father who didn't treat his mom well, so he didn't have a good example of how to love."*
- *"He is wounded, so he is lashing out at me from a place of pain."*
- *"He's just scared. It's fear that is beneath his anger."*
- *"She's tired and under a lot of stress."*
- *"He is insecure. That's why he is treating me this way.*

Excusing their hurtful behaviors kept us in an abusive relationship and kept them completely unaccountable for their deplorable acts. It is time for us individually and as a society to stop making excuses for abusive behavior.

All of us are affected by the childhoods we experienced. Here is the thing: not all people who are wounded abuse. Some of the kindest people I know come from very abusive backgrounds, both physically and emotionally. I know many people who experienced horrendous trauma in their childhood on several different levels and did not grow up to be narcissists. In fact, most of them are wonderful people who treat others with kindness and respect. They make this world a better place.

Whatever the reason for a narcissist's abuse, the fact is CNs are bullies who ruin people's lives, and that is not okay.

Let's say they are acting out of their childhood wounds—does this mean it is okay for you to be their punching bag? Are you helping them or anyone else by being a recipient of their abuse? No, not ever.

Most CNs are not interested in getting help. They are not interested in healing, and they do not think they have a problem. So for us to spend countless hours trying to figure out why they are the way they are isn't helping them or us because there is no way of knowing for sure. We will just further exhaust ourselves, which after what we have been through, is the last thing we need.

It is time to let them own their own issues, their own feelings. You are not responsible for their actions. You also are not responsible for their feelings, even though they will tell you that you are. You are not an unkind person if you let them heal themselves or go to someone else to heal. You are not here to take abuse from anyone. When we let go of trying to figure out the why, we let go of them. Then we are left with ourselves, which at first can feel lonely. We are so used to being intertwined with them because when we love, we love deeply with all our heart.

But the more we go inside and take care of our own wounded heart, the stronger we will feel and the more peace we will experience. Life will take on a different feeling, and we will discover people like us, others who love authentically, with their whole heart.

When we let go of the drama of the why, we are one step closer to freedom and feeling whole again.

Is Their Abusive Behavior Conscious or Unconscious?

Many survivors wonder about this, partly because of cognitive dissonance, which I will explain a bit in the chapter on healing. It is so difficult to imagine that someone we thought loved us was (and is) consciously abusing us. This question, in my opinion, does not have a clear answer. There are some CNs I've known who feel more innocent while others seem diabolical and dark.

In some ways, they are not conscious because they do not live consciously. They are out of touch with who they really are. They have lost themselves, their soul identity. They are shells of their real self. But, on the other hand, judging, criticizing, and manipulating are conscious acts. The more jealous they get of you, the more they demean you. To belittle and demean is a conscious act.

There are professed narcissists who will explain exactly what they are thinking when they are manipulating someone. They are completely aware of what they are doing. I do think most CNs are more conscious and aware of what they are doing than we would like to imagine. It's just hard for our brains to accept this when we have seen them as they wanted us to see them for such a long time.

11

The Most Dangerous
Trait of All

One of the most concerning things I have observed about our society as a whole is that there is a growing number of people who lack empathy. This seems to be increasing, especially over the past couple of decades. As this planet has become more advanced in many ways, we are also losing what is most important. Having personally experienced the pain you have, I know you will understand this more than most. You are very valuable to this world because of what you've been through. You have insights that many don't.

Many of the political leaders running the world's countries are devoid of empathy, and this affects everything. In the United States where I live, we have two main political parties. I have observed overt and covert narcissistic behavior in both the Republican party and the Democratic party. Decisions made by political leaders, as well as heads of large corporations, affect all of us. If these are made from a place where empathy does not reside, it will not end well. When empathy isn't present in leadership, decisions are made that hold money and power as the greatest priority instead of the people who reside here and the planet that feeds and shelters us.

People with no empathy have no remorse and act out of their own selfishness, hurting others and not feeling badly about it. They excuse their destructive behavior and blame others. Covert narcissism is all around us, affecting our self-image and self-worth. This is even exemplified by corporations. When companies advertise products by giving us the message that we don't look as we should, and that if we buy their product, we will be more beautiful and acceptable, they are gaslighting us, demeaning us, and not treating us with kindness and respect, all for their own gain.

Be it personal or professional, when someone doesn't have empathy, there is a disconnection from their spirit. Our spirit, our soul, is our lifeforce. This is what drives us, what gives us purpose and meaning, what prompts us to love and to heal. It is what makes us a whole person. It is our true identity.

On a recent visit to England, I was walking up High Street in front of Windsor Castle. I was taking in the sights even though I didn't really feel like it. Just before I left for my trip, I received word of things one of the CNs in my life was doing to smear my name to people I love. It hit me hard and sent me into a state of mild depression. I felt numb as I walked alongside hundreds of other tourists down the busy sidewalk lined with shops and restaurants. I passed by a homeless woman sitting on the ground with a container in front of her holding different types of coins. Something stopped me in the flow of the crowd. I turned around, walked back a few feet, and asked, *"May I sit by you?"* She looked up, a bit shocked at the unusual request, and said, *"Sure!"*

I sat by her for a while. I asked her about her story, what brought her to where she was that day. She told me of growing up in West London, being kicked out by her abusive father and being on the streets ever since. Her body looked like it had experienced a lot of trauma for many years. Life had beaten her down, and she didn't have it in her to try anymore. I felt a kinship with her. Our paths were different, but I could easily be her. We had both experienced pain and life-sucking trauma. We had both felt the strength inside us slowly diminish. There was no one else I wanted to be talking to in that moment but her.

Sitting there looking at all the passersby, I was bothered by the fact I live in a world where hundreds of people from all different continents walked by her every day, choosing to buy mostly useless items that they would someday get rid of instead of doing something to help this woman. It bothered me that we live in a world where we have become numb to other people's pain. I am part of this world, and I have been one of those people walking by for far too long.

After our long conversation, I asked if I could give her some money and a hug. She smiled softly. I held her and said, *"I'm so sorry. I'm sorry for how hard life is for you right now. Lots of love to you today."* She embraced me back and said, *"Thank you for being so kind."* Empathy is what will change this world. Empathy is what heals. Empathy is what enables us to experience real connection with each other. Empathy is what allows us to see the things that really matter.

When someone doesn't have empathy, it is almost like they have a black hole inside of them. They don't have that warm core spark of life within them. As a result, they cannot ever fully feel the magic of a sunset, the feeling of real connection, or the transcendent experience of real love. Someone without empathy is in survival mode. They end up feeding off other people's energy because they are devoid of it. They find people who have life, who have connection, who have empathy and real love, then drain them of their own supply of energy. This is why the CN in your life chose you, and this is why he or she moved on to someone else so quickly.

If a CN were alone on a deserted island, they would waste away. People like you have what CNs want. They will never be able to sit with themselves and feel the peace that resides in all our spirits and souls. They are not capable of feeling the richness inside themselves like you are because they are devoid of life-giving energy. This can feel like a bleak picture, but here is the good news:

You are on this planet. You have empathy. You have a light in you that brings energy to this world. Because you were targeted by a CN for your empathetic heart, this may make you want to hide this light so you don't get hurt again. I completely understand that. It's part of your body trying to protect you.

Here is the thing. Your spirit is strong. You are educating yourself. You now know that you can trust your own inner guidance. You will be able to recognize the traits of people who will drain you. There is no reason to fear and every reason to love. There are people in this world who will see your pearls and so appreciate who you are and what you bring. They won't drain you of your lifeforce. In fact, you will feel even more life energy when you open your heart and love them.

You will learn to fortify boundaries with energy vampires and use your tender heart to reach out to those who gratefully receive it. Your heart will expand even more, and a newfound strength will develop in you that can move mountains.

You make this world a better place, and I'm so grateful to walk next to you.

12

Your Body Knew: Common Illnesses

When talking to survivors, I noticed there were some common illnesses that many of them experienced when they were in a relationship with a CN or being raised by one.

The *Secret Language of Your Body* by Inna Segal is a book to which I refer often for others and has been helpful for me. The author lists illnesses and bodily conditions, then talks about possible emotional causes for these symptoms or diseases. I've looked up various conditions that I've had, my kids have had, and friends of mine have had. I have been amazed at how incredibly accurate her book has been over many years.

Our bodies are intelligent and speak to us all the time. The body knows before the conscious mind. Many studies have confirmed this truth. One such study shared by Malcolm Gladwell in his book *"Blink: The Power of Thinking Without Thinking"* was done at The University of Iowa where a group of scientists conducted an experiment where they put four decks of cards in front of students. Two of the decks were red, and the other two were blue. Each card either won them money or cost them money. It was set up as a simple gambling game. The job of the student was to turn over cards from any of the decks, one at a time with the goal of gaining as much money as possible. What the students didn't know was the red decks were downfall decks. The rewards are high, but when you lose, you lose big. The blue decks had more gradual wins and losses with modest gains and losses. The scientists wanted to see how long it would take for the students to figure this out.

What they found was that after turning over roughly 50 cards, most students started to have a hunch that something was plotted. After picking up about 80 cards, most of them had figured out the difference between the decks of cards. The experiment was straightforward except for one fascinating twist. The scientists had hooked up each student to a machine that measured the activity of the sweat glands below the skin in the palms of their hands. Here is the eye-opening part: the scientists found that the gamblers' palms started sweating as a stress response by the tenth card! Also, around the tenth card their behavior also started to change. They started to organically choose the blue cards over the red. The students' unconscious minds had figured out the game before their conscious minds became aware of the differences.

During the time you were with a CN, your body knew before your conscious mind became aware of the truth of this person and the disguised abuse you were experiencing. The card game was simple, though living with a CN is the furthest thing from simple. The experiment is a great illustration of how much we can trust our body's responses. Often, those responses manifest as physical or mental illness, like depression.

When I asked men and women what type of physical and mental illnesses they had experienced over the course of the relationship with the CN, there were many common conditions. I asked if they wanted me to read the possible emotional reasons for the physical conditions they had experienced. As I read from Segal's book, each survivor was amazed at what they heard. Some were brought to tears. What I read was exactly how they had felt in the relationship.

Here are some examples, with excerpts from Segal's book, *The Secret Language of Your Body*:

After about a year of dating her CN, Dana developed a severe case of candida. When I read what her body was trying to tell her at the time, she couldn't believe it.

- *Self-doubt.*
- *Feeling scattered, hazy, frazzled, stressed, trapped.*
- *Frustrated with partner.*
- *Difficulty trusting.*

When she considered the descriptions, she was feeling all of those things at the time, but had explained them all away because he was such a "great guy." Everyone around her loved him and was constantly confirming how lucky she was. The trap of the powerful love-bombing stage had been laid, so she trusted the way he appeared more than things she was feeling deep inside. She excused things he did that were unkind and disrespectful, believing he loved and cared about her. Her body knew better and was trying to warn her. She was feeling stressed and trapped for a reason. She had difficulty trusting him because her body knew he could not be trusted. She didn't realize how much she could trust herself.

Jane was raised by a CN mom. She had chronic strep throat beginning at a young age. The probable emotional causes were clear.

- *Anger, rage, hurt, hatred.*
- *Feeling inferior.*
- *Don't know how to stand up for yourself, even though you are burning inside.*

These were all things Jane felt growing up.

Urinary tract infections were common among women in romantic relationships with CNs. The probable emotional reasons:

- *Carrying a tremendous amount of guilt and fear.*
- *A deep-seated belief that there is something wrong with you.*
- *Allowing people to manipulate and control you.*
- *Sexual pressure and shame.*

The body is amazing. It knows first. The women were all stunned when I read about their illnesses. Their bodies had validated everything they had felt at the time. Other conditions I came across in my interviews were fibromyalgia, headaches, anxiety, asthma, and chronic fatigue.

Part of the healing process is learning to trust yourself. When you are in a relationship with a CN, this is something that is suppressed in you. They lie and manipulate, but appear loving and innocent; this makes trusting your own feelings as well as your body very difficult and perplexing. What they say sounds smart and reasonable, but your body is telling you something else.

The truth is that you are your best barometer for truth. Your body is here to help you, to guide you.

When you reflect on all the physical symptoms you experienced when you were with a CN and read the probable emotional causes, you will see how incredibly brilliant your body is. It knew before you did.

13

What Survivors Feel

As I listened to survivors share how they felt while they were in a relationship with a CN, and how they feel as they uncover the truth, I noticed many common thoughts, fears, and emotions among them. I thought it would be helpful to share some of these with you to validate your own experience, so you can see you are not alone.

Here is a list of common things victims told me they felt when they were in a relationship with a CN:

- *"I felt like the CN was interesting and I was dull."*
- *"I felt judged for the dumbest things."*
- *"I felt like things about me were irritating to her."*
- *"I felt like I was too quiet, too loud, too opinionated, too strong, too lazy, too picky, and not easygoing enough."*
- *"I felt stifled, held down for years."*
- *"I didn't feel free to be myself, all of me."*
- *"I felt needy when I was around him."*
- *"I felt insecure."*

- *"I felt like I was an object that was easily replaceable."*
- *"It felt like he was the positive one and I was the downer."*
- *"I felt like I was too emotional, too sensitive, too much for her."*
- *"I didn't feel valued and pursued."*
- *"I didn't feel like he wanted me to thrive."*
- *"I felt stripped of confidence, happiness, joy, and excitement for life."*
- *"I felt like a failure."*
- *"I felt like the way I parented irritated her."*
- *"I felt like so many things were wrong with me."*
- *"I felt like I didn't deserve love."*
- *"I felt like I was never good enough."*
- *"I felt like there was no way to win his approval."*
- *"I had a lot of self-doubt."*
- *"I felt not considered."*
- *"My self-worth went really low."*
- *"I felt old, tired, weathered."*
- *"I felt depleted."*
- *"I felt a lot of anxiety."*
- *"I never felt thin enough or pretty enough."*
- *"I never felt like I wore the right clothes."*
- *"I felt lifeless, drained."*

Here are some things survivors said they feel now as they discover the truth about their CN spouse/parent/boss:

- *"Low-level depression."*
- *"I feel such deep grief like I've never felt before and I find myself crying uncontrollably at times."*
- *"So angry."*

- *"I feel alone, even though I have family and friends that support me."*
- *"Sometimes I wonder if I'll ever feel happy. I look at people laughing, enjoying themselves, and wonder if I'll ever feel that."*
- *"The more my eyes are opening the lighter I am feeling."*
- *"It's hard to imagine ever being in a relationship that is the real thing, to actually be loved by someone who wants nothing from me, but simply enjoys me and truly loves me."*
- *"I feel suspicious of new people I meet, not knowing who I can trust."*
- *"I feel scared about the future, not confident that I will be able to make it in this world on my own."*
- *"I'm feeling a lot of self-doubt."*
- *"I haven't had a good night's sleep in years."*
- *"There are days I find myself entertaining thoughts of leaving this planet. It all feels like too much, and it makes me want to not be here anymore. It all feels too hard and too painful."*
- *"I'm tired a lot."*
- *"My self-confidence is low."*
- *"I feel misunderstood. I try to explain the relationship to friends, and it never sounds that bad when I say it out loud. Then I question myself and feel even more despair and loneliness."*
- *"I stay home a lot. I don't feel like being social."*
- *"I find it hard to date other people because I no longer trust 'the nicest people.' It's also hard to trust myself to choose someone who is healthy. I doubt my own discernment because of everything I've been through."*
- *"I've been overeating a lot which makes me feel even worse about myself."*
- *"I have no desire to eat."*

- *"I feel discouraged because he seems so happy and I'm still falling apart."*
- *"I feel like I am always bracing myself for the next angry phone call, email, or text from him. I have symptoms of PTSD like flashbacks, depression, anxiety, withdrawal, emotional numbing, reliving different events, and feelings of guilt and shame."*
- *"I'm so used to being sabotaged by this person, it's like I am constantly waiting for the ball to drop."*
- *"I am starting to feel more hope."*
- *"I am beginning to feel stronger."*
- *"The other day I got an angry email from my ex, and I noticed I felt the same trauma I always feel but I was able to move on faster this time."*
- *"I'm beginning to dream again and starting to actually feel excited about my future."*
- *"I'm feeling really grateful to be out of that relationship and have the space to heal."*

As you heal, you will find yourself going through waves of different emotions. Some days you will feel discouraged, and other days you will feel hope. You might feel like you are moving on, feeling stronger. Then you see the CN or receive an email or a phone call from them that sends you into a state of emotional paralysis. You find you can't function. It takes time to get back to your center.

You have been through a tremendously difficult and painful experience. You have been treated terribly by someone who is selfish and doesn't care about you. You have been given messages about who you are that are not true. You have been conned, manipulated, lied to, and brainwashed. You have been belittled, talked down to, and treated with disrespect. You were used. You have been emotionally and psychologically abused for years.

You have been blamed for things that had nothing to do with you. You have been made to feel like things are wrong with you when they are not. You have been treated in a way that has made you doubt yourself. Someone who does not have your best interests at heart has controlled you. You have experienced the illusion of love, not the real thing. Not even close.

Because of their manipulation, you have received the damaging message that you are not worthy of kindness, love, and respect. You now wonder if you are even worthy of enjoying this life.

You did not deserve any of this even though you have been made to think you did. Your mind, your body, and your heart need abundant kindness and tenderness now so you can find your way home.

It is important that you know this was abuse. You thought it was love because they acted like it was; said it was. The truth is you are a survivor of abuse. You have no physical scars, so it is easy and common to underplay what you have been through, but the reality is you are a victim and survivor of psychological and emotional abuse.

You have been through enough, and now it is time to heal and restore the truth of how beautiful and valuable you are. You are kind, genuine, loving, tender, and strong. This is the truth of who you are. You are full of life. I know you haven't felt that for a while, if ever. You have a light in you that has been temporarily dimmed. That bright life buried inside you is ready to emerge.

You will feel that beautiful smile again. You won't always be in this valley. You are forging steps to climb out. You will make it to the top where you will feel fresh, clean air that will fill your traumatized body with love, real love that feels amazing.

This is what you are born to feel. You are made for love, and it is time to come back to who you really are.

14

The Road to Healing
and Restoration

When you are in a relationship with a covert narcissist, parts of you shut down. You lose sight of the truth of who you are. The life inside you is not there like it used to be. Your heart has been deeply wounded and betrayed. You feel devastated.

You may feel like a mess inside. The truth is you are not a mess. You have experienced evil. Your body is having a natural reaction to that. You were made for love, to be loved, to feel love, and to share love. You lived with the opposite, and everything you feel is a result of that and makes complete sense.

When I brought up the subject of healing and restoration to one survivor I interviewed, she said, *"Do you think that is even possible?"*

I want you to know, as I told her, healing is absolutely possible. Your heart and your body deserve it. You have been through a lot. You will be amazed by the strength and hope and love that you will experience as you heal.

One of the things necessary for healing to take place is recognizing the truth of the relationship and that person. You experienced so many covert lies; it is incredibly helpful to be able to see clearly.

The truth is you were in love with an illusion, with the person they portrayed themselves to be. At first, this is an excruciating realization. You will doubt and wonder if you are overinflating this, if they really are innocent and you're just scared to move on. You will have a ton of self-doubt. Eventually, with education and support, you will see that your hunch, your inner knowing, is on target. In time the truth that you were in love with an illusion will feel like a relief because truth does set you free. That full realization will validate years of confusion you felt, years of unexplained exhaustion and health issues, years of sexual confusion, years of feeling less than, and years of unhappiness, along with anxiety.

You lived in an unsafe environment, were demeaned and devalued for years (decades for some of you; entire childhoods for many of you). You did not experience unconditional love; you did not live with someone who treated you with respect, who cherished you, treasured you, and felt so lucky to have you in their life.

No, the truth is you experienced a counterfeit.

If this was a spouse or romantic partner, this awakening to the truth is excruciating because you did love that person with all your heart. You were dedicated. You were in 100%.

The truth is that you were the lifeforce in the relationship. When you're really honest with yourself, when you look back with clear vision, that life, that love you gave and felt, was never fully reciprocated.

It is painful and confusing to be cut off so quickly and harshly by someone you genuinely loved. Any feelings you thought they had for you are vanished, and instead, you experience a person who hates you and sees you as the enemy, and blames you for things that make no rational sense. At the same time, they are making sure their world always looks greener and more wonderful than yours. They move on quickly and make sure to let you know how much happier they are without you.

The truth is this relationship never meant the same to them as it did to you. You approached it from a genuine, goodhearted, loving place. They did not. They acted like they did, but it wasn't genuine. The reality is they have enormous issues and have projected them onto you for years, making you think you are responsible for things that have nothing to do with you.

A big part of healing is recognizing the truth and coming to the place where you can accept that it really was all an illusion. This takes time and can't be forced. Accepting what really happened is a natural result that comes with educating yourself on covert narcissism, getting support, and learning to trust yourself and treat yourself with the utmost love and kindness.

You Were Abused

The Merriam-Webster Dictionary online defines verbal abuse as, *"Language that condemns or vilifies, usually unjustly, intemperately, and angrily."* Psychology Today, in an article titled "When Is It Emotional Abuse?" defined emotional abuse as:

> *...an attempt to control, in just the same way that physical abuse is an attempt to control another person. The only difference is that the emotional abuser does not use physical hitting, kicking, pinching, grabbing, pushing or other physical forms of harm. Rather the perpetrator of emotional abuse uses emotion as his/her weapon of choice.*

Emotional abuse in our culture is pervasive and damaging, and it's as relevant a topic as physical and sexual abuse. Emotional abuse undercuts a person's foundational self-confidence and love of self and replaces them with confusion about self-worth, value, justice, mercy, and love.

It is easy to diminish what you experienced because no one hit you physically or sexually abused you. It is common for victims to wonder if they are blowing their experience out of proportion or overdramatizing it. They often see themselves as the one to blame. This is what the CN wants. They do things to distract you and throw you off of seeing the truth. So many victims stay quiet because they don't feel they have the right to call it abuse. It is such a strong word that we generally associate with bruises and visible scars, with yelling and screaming.

A covert narcissist is in some ways a more dangerous abuser. I say this delicately. All abusers are horrific, and all abuse is deplorable; all victims of all types of abuse have been through a tremendous amount. I don't want to diminish anyone's pain. The point I'm trying to make is when someone is hitting you or yelling at you it is clearly abuse. Covert abuse is hidden and so subtle, it is far from obvious. Manipulative, covert tactics not only hurt you, they also chip away at your identity, your self-worth, and make you feel like this is all your fault.

Covert emotional and psychological abuse is what happens in cults. Leaders who make you feel loved can also talk you into committing suicide. These people are powerful. Do not diminish what you have experienced. You have been controlled and manipulated for years. You are a victim of abuse. You are also an incredibly strong survivor because you are still here and you are reading this book, which tells me a lot about you. It tells me you are smart, a researcher, and a deep thinker. You are strong because even through your tears and confusion you are looking for answers. I also know that because you have all that as your core, you are going to come out of this just fine, even better than you could imagine.

Keep going. We need people like you in this world. Don't let this take you out. You are the cream of the crop. You are the type of person who makes this planet a better place. Thank you for being brave, for being you.

Cognitive Dissonance

Cognitive dissonance is when you hold two conflicting beliefs in your mind. The Merriam-Webster Dictionary defines it as, *"Psychological conflict resulting from incongruous beliefs and attitudes held simultaneously."* This is what makes covert narcissistic abuse so confusing and difficult. For so long you believed this person was kind and genuine. You believed with all your heart this person loved and cared about you. When you start to experience cruelty from them that is more overt or when you begin to discover they have many narcissistic traits, this messes with your mind because seeing them as manipulative and controlling contrasts the belief that they are loving, kind, and innocent.

When you hold a belief strongly, it is difficult to believe something that is so contrary to it, even if the evidence is undeniable and staring you in the face. When you start opening your eyes to ways the CN has controlled, manipulated, belittled, and demeaned you for years, this is a huge reality paradigm shift. You will fight hard against the evidence no matter how obvious it is. This stirs up great insecurity, confusion, and anxiety in the body. What makes it even harder is that people around you see the CN in a positive light.

Cognitive dissonance is one of the most challenging components of healing and recovery. It takes enormous mental strength to look past strong beliefs you have held and be open to looking honestly at the reality that is presenting itself.

With time, education, and support, your eyes will open more and more. The stronger you become in yourself, and the more you treat yourself with profound love, you will begin to see what really happened. Your brain will do a lot of shifting and analyzing. The brain looks for evidence to support beliefs. It is helpful to talk through events in your mind, retraining it to see truth from different angles.

This healing process is challenging. It takes effort on your part, but it is so worth it. It will change you in ways that bring about such strength and clarity that other areas in your life will also be affected, in a profound and beautiful way.

This Was Not Your Fault

It is so easy to get caught up in the thinking this was your fault, for two reasons. First, the CN in your life is constantly telling you that or inferring it. Also, you are a self-reflective person who takes responsibility for your actions, not wanting to blame other people. With respect to what has happened with the CN, I can tell you the way you were treated was not your fault. Your beautiful traits were exploited and used to harm you, to make you question yourself.

> *"You were manipulated, insulted, degraded, belittled, and neglected. Full responsibility for this goes to the psychopath.*

It does not matter if you were vulnerable or insecure—no decent human being should ever take advantage of another. None of this was your fault" (Jackson MacKenzie, Psychopath Free).

That is what happened. You can let go of self-blame and focus on self-love. You have been blamed enough for probably ridiculous things. It is time now to see the truth of how special you are. Allow yourself to believe the ones who actually love you. Let go of the ones whose actions do not match their words. Let go of the illusions, the manipulators. Spend your time with the ones who sincerely love you and want the best for you. Allow yourself to feel that love. Breathe it in and let it permeate every part of you. You are beginning a new life where love exists, and everything else must leave.

The Healing Progression

As you unfold the truth and deprogram yourself from the lies, you will experience ups and downs on your way back home to yourself. Mary remembers this happening to her. She was feeling great, working toward her goals, building a new life, and then an email came. It was a three-page assault of her character filled with lies and manipulation. It flattened her. She cried on and off the next few days. She felt paralyzed and numb, and slipped into despair. She couldn't think clearly. She thought she was doing so well. She was. The progress she did see is that she bounced back faster this time compared to times in the past with her ex.

Time went on. Mary had good, strong days, and also days of despair, loneliness, and anxiety, but she kept going to her support group and doing healing exercises. Then one day she called to tell me about a significant breakthrough. She stumbled upon an old journal when she was cleaning up and decided to read the part that took place during her divorce. She found a list she had written down of all the cruel things her CN ex had told her were "wrong" with her. For years, she had mentally reviewed these. They had affected her greatly. For a long time, she questioned herself and wondered if they were true about her and she just didn't see it. That day when she found the list, she didn't feel the same anxiety and sinking feeling she had been used to feeling. This time she looked at the list and felt almost completely unfazed. She went through each one and thought, *That's so not true. That's not even close to who I am.* Then she took a closer look and was able to clearly see that most of these things he said about her were, in fact, true of him.

There was something else that struck her. *This was all so mean, all these things he had said to me*, she thought. For so long she had just focused on the thought, *What if he's right? What if these are really true about me?* She was stronger now, and able to see clearly because she had been educating herself, spending her time treating herself with more kindness and respect, as well as surrounding herself with people who treated her with real love. She was now in a place where she was so used to experiencing authentic love that meanness and bullying was starting to feel foreign to her.

This was a massive breakthrough. Mary even looks different from when I first met her. Many of her friends have commented that she looks 10 years younger. That's what healing does, what love does, what not being in a toxic relationship does.

One thing to notice is that CNs will tell you what is wrong with you. Targets don't do that. Targets say things like, *"When you said that, I felt this…"* CNs are not reflective people and are emotionally immature. They blame others; they don't take responsibility for themselves, but instead project their own issues onto others.

I hope Mary's story encourages you. Know that you will go up and down, but you are making progress and someday will see very clearly to the point that the words your CN uses won't affect you anymore. You will absolutely know the truth of who you are and no one will be able to take that from you again.

A Healing Exercise

I gave Mary different exercises to do that helped her heal. One of them helped enable her breakthrough. The first time she did this exercise she found it difficult, but each time she revisited it, the truth was easier for her to see.

Here is the exercise for you to do if you would like:

1. Write a list of everything the covert narcissist in your life said is wrong with you. This may be what was directly told to you, or was insinuated.

_____

_____

_____

_____

_____

_____

2. Now look back over the list and ask yourself with each one if this is really true about *you*. If you are feeling a lot of confusion right now and have a hard time thinking clearly at this point of your recovery, ask a trusted friend who knows you well if any of these are true about you. Also, if they are true, is it a big deal? Is it really something that is wrong with you? For instance, Mary's ex put her down for being overweight. Is that something that is wrong with who she is? *No.*

3. After answering if each one is true about you, go back over each statement of what is "wrong with you" according to Mr. or Ms. Toxic and ask if these statements are actually true of the CN who said them. The clearer you get, you will be amazed at how many are projections of who the CN is and that the putdowns have nothing to do with you.

4. Now, write below the truth of who you are. Make a list of all the beautiful characteristics about yourself to help as a reminder of who you really are. If you have a hard time coming up with characteristics, ask a friend who knows you well to help you with this.

_____

_____

_____

_____

_____

Blaming Yourself

Because of the way CNs treat their victims, it is easy to think you are at fault for so many things that have nothing to do with you. I want you to know that no matter what you did or think you could have done, there is no way this relationship could have thrived. Because covert narcissists do not have empathy, are self-focused, use people, and do not take responsibility for their actions, it is impossible for anyone to have a healthy relationship with them.

Loving, healthy, life-giving relationships require certain essential traits, such as putting yourself in the other person's shoes, showing respect, really listening, caring about the other person's feelings, being self-reflective, and wanting the best for the other person. The relationship can only work if both people have these traits.

What Does Love Actually Look Like?

When you live with a CN for a long time, toxic behavior becomes your new normal. You lose touch with how love is really supposed to look and feel.

It is important and helpful to get in touch with what the real thing looks like. One way of doing this is looking at the relationships you do have that are consistently loving. Jackson MacKenzie calls these people your "constants" in his book, *Psychopath Free*. I love that. It's a great term! These are the people in your life who are consistent. They have loved you for years. You feel safe with them; you feel unconditionally loved by them because you are. If you don't have anyone like this, your constant might be an animal you take care of or how you feel watching a sunset, sitting by the ocean, or standing on top of a mountain.

Think of someone who is your constant. Do you ever feel discombobulated around them? Does your stomach ever tighten when you are with them? Do they ever tell you all the things they think are wrong with you? When you are with them, do you feel like they enjoy you? Is it easy to think clearly around them? Do you ever feel belittled or demeaned by them? Are you ever in a pile of your own tears after being with them? Do you question yourself and doubt yourself when you are with them?

My best friend in the world is Liz. We met in school around the age of twelve. We talk on the phone almost every week and have for the last 28 years. We talk about everything under the sun. She is gold. She is stunning. Her heart is as big and as vast as they come. She is one of my constants. I have only experienced unconditional love and acceptance from her. We have cried with each other many times, talked about life, our kids, our relationships. We call each other when we are angry and sad and excited, and both feel safe to let out whatever we are feeling and whatever we are thinking. No matter what I am going through, she wants to know. My feelings matter to her.

Liz wants the best for me. I feel her enjoyment of me. We laugh a lot. I am able to think clearly whenever we talk; in fact, many times I call her when I am confused about something and by the end of the call I feel clear. I have never felt judged or put down by her. We both have mad respect for each other. She is a barometer for me of what love looks and feels like, and that alone has been so helpful in my own journey of healing.

My mom is another constant. She passed away a few years ago, but I carry all loving memories of her with me daily. She was the personification of unconditional love. I always felt fully accepted by her. I don't ever remember her putting me down through her words or in any other way. She never gave me the silent treatment, never belittled me, and didn't try to control or manipulate me. She believed in me wholeheartedly. Her number-one priority was to give my dear sister and me a foundation of love, and she did a beautiful job of that. Her heart was always available to me. My feelings mattered to her. She had such empathy and gave the warmest hugs that let me know she really, truly, and sincerely cared. If she did something that hurt or affected someone else, she took responsibility and apologized. Not a fake apology, a sincere one. I never felt drained by her. I felt calmed and reassured. She loved who I was, and I felt it. I felt safe with her.

I share these stories to help illustrate how vastly different real love looks compared to the twisted illusion you have experienced, to give you a reference point for love. When someone loves you, sincerely loves you, your body feels calmed. You don't feel anxiety when you are with them. You feel relief. It is so important for us to know what the real thing looks like and feels like.

When we see real love demonstrated, it helps us recognize the reality of the mess we had in our lives. It helps us see that it was all words with no actions to match.

Be that love for yourself and surround yourself with more and more constants. Eventually, you will become one of your own constants. When you start feeling that coming from yourself, it is a life-changer. That's when inner peace really starts to settle in, and the new life you are creating begins to feel magical.

Traits of Real Love

- They treat you with respect.
- They stand up for you.
- They believe in you.
- They listen to you.
- They really know you.
- They respect your feelings.
- They want you to be happy.
- Sex—they cherish you, love your body, and love to give you pleasure.
- They love to treat you and celebrate you.
- They value you.
- They enjoy you.
- They treat you with kindness.
- They support you in your endeavors.
- They feel excited for you when you succeed.
- They feel empathy for you when you feel sad, scared, and unsure.
- Their honesty comes from a place of love.
- They want the best for you.
- They defend you to others.
- They care about you.
- They trust and respect your instincts.
- They encourage you.
- They truly love you, not just with their words, but also their actions.

Becoming the Safest Place Possible

When you live with a covert narcissist, you are not with someone who is emotionally safe. Because of this, you learn to doubt yourself and to not see your happiness as being just as important as theirs. You are encouraged by them to not listen and not trust your own instincts. Your heart is not protected or loved.

A big part of healing is learning how to give all of that to yourself. We often hear from self-help books and speakers that we need to love ourselves. But what does that look like in real life? After being with someone who has devalued you for years, it takes time to learn how to treat yourself in a way that is loving and honoring of your heart.

I went through my own healing process and learned how to create the safest place possible inside of me. The more I changed the way I treated myself and my perspective on certain things, the more my life changed in ways I didn't even anticipate when I started on this healing journey. The more I treated myself with kindness and love, the less tolerant I became of other people who treated me badly and the more I was able to see through people. I also noticed that the critical voice inside myself left. Life began to feel different in the best ways possible. I have a connection with myself now that I did not have before.

I wrote about my own healing journey in my first book, *The Safest Place Possible: A Guide to Healing and Restoration.* The information and personal stories in this book will give you gentle tools to heal and restore your tender heart. In it I explain exercises I used that helped restore me to the woman I was inside all along.

You deserve so much love, and the freedom to be the beautiful, whole person you truly are. This process of healing will change your life in so many amazing ways. I know this may be hard to imagine right now, but I've been where you are, and there is truly light at the end of this dark tunnel. You will get there, and I can't wait to someday meet you and hear your story.

Physical Nurturing

When you live with a CN, not only is your heart affected, but your physical body is, as well. You experience emotional trauma, and your memories are stored in your body. Another part of healing is recognizing the truth of this and treating yourself to healing modalities such as massage, reiki, TRE, and masturbation. Did that last one surprise you? Let's talk about that one first.

If you were in a romantic relationship with a CN, sex was probably not good. You most likely felt confused, not good enough, and wounded. It probably affected your self-esteem and self-worth. This is an area to heal, and one way of doing this is being what you needed for yourself, awakening that part of you. You are a sexual being and have been starved of the beauty and fun of it. It's time to explore your amazing body and get in touch with that sexiness that was shut down by the CN. It is also a physical release to bring yourself to orgasm. You actually release oxytocin when you climax, which makes you feel more content, safe, and relaxed. It brings you back to yourself. Use candles, music, whatever feels delicious to you. Learn your body, what makes it feel great. You deserve to feel great. This will help you establish the truth that your body is beautiful, desirable, and worthy of pleasure. Doing this will also help get rid of any shame you are carrying from the toxic person you were with. Take time to meet your luscious, sexy self, and love yourself with every fiber of your being.

Next, if you haven't heard of TRE, it is worth the research. See if there are any places that facilitate TRE in your area. If not, this is something you can do on your own. TRE stands for "trauma release exercises." In a session, you do a series of exercises that help the body release deep muscular patterns of stress, tension, and trauma. After safely bringing your muscles to fatigue, your body automatically starts shaking as you lie in a certain position on the floor. This releases trauma in the body and calms your nervous system. While you are lying down, you allow your body to shake for about 20 minutes. When you are done, you will be amazed how much more calm and peaceful you feel. Your body does all the work for you. This process was created by Dr. David Berceli, Ph.D. There are many articles online, books, and YouTube videos if you would like to know more. This is a powerful and effective way of releasing trauma from the body.

In addition, reiki helps calm your body and spirit. It helps you feel more relaxed and reminds the body how it feels to be calm again. When the noise of all our fearful thoughts gets quieted, and our spirit feels peace, physical healing of the body can begin. Because you have experienced covert trauma over a long period of time, having a fight-or-flight response is common. Emotions are often buried during the relationship to help you get through it. These emotions can get trapped and stored in your body as cellular memory. Reiki helps you relax so the trapped emotions and trauma can gently be released.

I also recommend massage with a well-trained and sensitive practitioner. Walking and being in nature is soothing to the soul, as well. Whatever helps bring you calm and peace will allow your body to heal emotionally as well as physically. Retreats are a good place to go for self-care, which is a big part of healing. Treat yourself. Invest in you. You will begin to see how deserving you are of things that bring you calm, as well as how necessary it is for your wellbeing.

Boundaries

If you are able to, the best thing to do with covert narcissists is to have no contact with them. Because they are manipulative and know what triggers and affects you, if you have any contact with them, you are putting yourself in a vulnerable position to be injured emotionally again and again. The more you are away from them, the clearer the truth will be. Just like coming out of a cult, you need to completely get away to be able to get stronger in yourself. You can use technology to your advantage and block the CN's cell phone number and email address.

If you share kids with a CN, no contact may not be possible, depending on the children's ages. If this is the case, I suggest only communicating through email and text messages, not face to face. Seeing them will affect you and you need time and space to heal. I would also just stick to facts and planning issues, keeping personal thoughts and feelings to yourself. If you open up to them, if you are vulnerable in any way, they will hurt you, and that's the last thing you need. Protect your heart and share your thoughts and feelings with a trusted friend, counselor, or coach. This is a time to really look out for yourself just like you would for your kids or good friends.

Emotions

A lot of feelings are going to come up while you are healing. You will feel angry. You have been betrayed in such a brutal way. There are so many reasons for you to be angry. Allow yourself to be angry.

You will also feel grief. You are mourning the death of a spouse or parent you thought you had. If this was a marriage that is ending, you might have thought you were going to be married to this "wonderful" person for years. You had built a life with them. You might have kids together. This picture was your present and your future, and now it is gone. Allow yourself to grieve the loss.

You will feel sadness, ranging from low-level to deep depression. This is completely understandable. Allow yourself to feel sad. Many people tell me they are afraid if they cry they will never stop, so they don't allow themselves to feel the sadness. The opposite is actually true. If you don't release the tears, they will fester inside you. When you let yourself cry, your body gets to let go of what is ready to leave. Your body knows how to heal itself. It is incredibly smart. Listen to it. If you feel like crying, let it out. You won't always feel this sadness. It will become a thing of the past for you with time. Allow it to flow through you and be released out of you. It will bring you to freedom and indescribable peace.

When emotions rise, and we allow them to do so, we are recognizing the presence of something important that needs attention, and that is a beautiful picture of self-care.

When you were with the CN, your emotions were not valued. Now it is time to treat yourself with love and acceptance of every part of you. One way of doing that is honoring and respecting each and every feeling you have. Your inner self is important. You have experienced someone who gave you a different message. That was not love. You have another chance to show yourself what love really looks like. Let the emotions pass through you as they come. They are here to help you. It has helped me tremendously to make peace with and welcome every feeling that emerges.

It's easy to view ourselves as a mess when we are healing. I love the quote from *Love Warrior* by Glennon Doyle that says, *"You are not a mess. You are a feeling person in a messy world."*

This Experience Changes You

Because most victims are optimists, idealists, people who see the best in others, having someone you thought was kind and loving for years turn out to be a covert narcissist changes the way you see people. It can't help but do that. We tend to see people as the same as us. We don't assume people are controlling and manipulate because that isn't the way we think and behave. We believe people when they are kind, when they say they love us. We have no reason to not believe it.

If our loved ones are moody or say something or act in a way that feels confusing to us, we assume they are going through something, that they are dealing with some issue in or outside of themselves that is making them act this way. We want to love them, listen to them, and help heal whatever parts of them are wounded.

> *"We've been pre-programmed to believe that people only exhibit problem behaviors when they're 'troubled' inside or anxious about something. We usually start to wonder what's bothering the person so badly 'underneath' it all that's making them act in some disturbing way"* (George Simon Jr., Ph.D., *In Sheep's Clothing*).

I think it is true that narcissists are troubled people. They would not act the way they do if they weren't. What we learn through our experience is they are not always innocent. They are not coming from a naïve place. For the most part, they do what they do to get their way. We are waking up to the reality that there are people in the world who simply don't have good intentions, who are out for themselves and are not as they appear. There are bullies masquerading as the "nicest people" and no matter how kind and loving and understanding we are, they will treat us badly because they don't care about our feelings. They want what they want and will do what it takes to get their way. They do not care who they hurt in the process.

This world takes on a different feeling when you realize you can't always trust people according to how they act and appear to be. Your view of humanity as a whole begins to change when you start seeing how many people are posing as someone they are not. It is natural to want to retreat and want nothing to do with this world after what you've experienced. Sometimes we need to for a time in order to reconnect with ourselves and get our bearings.

At first, you'll feel sad. There is an innocence that is now gone, and once you have realizations in life, there really is no going back to your old self. I felt sad about this for a while, but that has changed for me. This was a wake-up call. For a long time, this realization made me want to retreat from society. I didn't know who I could trust anymore. Then I noticed this separation from humanity felt healthy and freeing. I was on the outside looking in more than in the middle of human drama. I started to feel stronger, clearer standing on my own observing the world around me. I was able to pull away and give myself space to breathe. When I began to involve myself with people again, I didn't just jump into trusting them, I noticed how I felt around them, and I trusted that. It was empowering.

I have become a lot more selective about those with whom I spend my time. The kind people, the genuine ones, have become even more precious to me and my heart has enlarged for the innocent ones. I feel stronger and even more compassionate than I used to be. I trust my discernment now more than ever because I am paying more attention to how I feel around someone, more than to what they are saying and how they are acting.

Your experience has changed you, but as you begin to emerge from the shadows of pain, the light of the goodness in others becomes so much brighter. What you have gone through is horrific, but because of what you have learned and experienced you have even more depth and layers than you did before. You can help others in a way that many people can't. You are gold. It is painful now, I know, but strength is coming.

Find Support

This is a time when you may want to isolate yourself and not reach out to people. I understand that. When I was educating myself and feeling so many overwhelming emotions, I didn't want to leave my house. I didn't want to talk to people. I just wanted to curl up in a corner and cry and stare at walls. I get it. I think there is a time for that, and that's okay. Listen to what your body and heart need.

As time passed, I started to reach out more for help. I went to therapists and quickly learned not all of them understand or are educated on the subject of covert narcissism. I narrowed my search of coaches and therapists to only those who focused on this area. Talking to them was very helpful.

Then I discovered support groups in the area. Sitting in a room with 20 other people sharing stories of what they had been through and were going through was eye-opening and incredibly helpful. I wasn't the only one! I couldn't believe how similar the stories were. I recognized myself in so many of them. We all felt an immediate kinship, a freedom, and safety. The biggest thing all of us wanted was to keep hearing and sharing stories. It is so validating to meet others who have gone through similar things. You understand each other immediately, and there is a safety you feel that is precious and so sacred.

When I decided to write this book, I wanted it to be helpful, accurate, and comprehensive, so I asked dozens of people if I could interview them about their experiences. My intention was to have a variety of experiences and stories to help as many people as possible. Every one of them said yes. They wanted to help in any way they could. Hearing them be vulnerable with me was humbling. I felt honored. It also fueled me even more to write this book.

As I conducted research, my eyes were opened to how big and vast a worldwide problem this is. I not only interviewed local people, but also others from around the world. The feelings and experiences were the same.

I highly recommend connecting with other people who have been through a relationship with a covert narcissist. You will not feel alone anymore. It will help you get to the truth and see through the lies and manipulation. This will help you heal and grow stronger.

You Can Trust Yourself

Many boundaries are crossed by a CN. Not trusting your gut is instilled in you from them. CNs do not respect your thoughts or intuition, which solidifies the message that you cannot trust your own feelings. When you brought up concerns to them, telling them how you were feeling, they would talk you out of your gut reactions, making you question if you can trust yourself. When you experience years of this, it becomes difficult to trust yourself again, and you find yourself doubting your own internal compass.

This is something to strengthen as you heal. One way of doing this is reading through old journals. Many survivors are amazed how much they did see about their CN, but at the time made excuses because they believed they had chosen a good person. Let this be an encouragement to you. You really can trust yourself.

If you didn't keep a journal throughout the years, another way to strengthen belief in yourself is to test your inner compass. When you are around people, begin noticing how your body feels. *Do you feel at ease? Do you feel good about yourself? Do you feel strengthened being around them, encouraged, empowered? Do you feel fearful? Anxious? Judged?*

Sometimes our assessment of why we are feeling the way we are isn't correct, but you can always trust that you are picking something up for a reason. You are not too sensitive, too dramatic, or reading into things. If your body has a reaction to someone, trust that reaction. Do not spend a lot of time with people who don't feel good to your body, especially as you are healing and getting stronger. The more you listen to your body, the more you will see how astute and enlightening it is.

Having experienced this, you will find yourself growing fierce about things you feel inside of you when someone is talking to you.

They may look lovely, act put-together, sound confident, say nice things, but your stomach rolls in warning. Something is off with this person. I encourage you to listen to that above all else. You now know people can put on the most convincing act and be completely different from the front they are showing. This is a very useful thing to know in life. You are now a person with a tender heart as well as a whole lot of wisdom. That is a powerful combination. One way to know for sure if someone is genuine is to pay attention to the signs of your body, what you are feeling inside.

You have the most accurate barometer for truth living within you. Every time you choose to trust yourself, you are strengthening a muscle that will someday become second nature.

This will trickle into every area of your life—relationships, career, everyday decisions, where to live, where to vacation, etc. You have a gold mine inside you, and the more you use it, trust it, believe in it, the more miracles you will experience. Life will take on a magical feeling. Things will seem to flow with more ease and enjoyment. Your life will unfold in a way where you feel incredibly loved because you are.

Permission to Be Strong

CNs, whether they are parents, spouses, or coworkers, give out the same messages: *"Something is wrong with you, and you will not be able to make it in this world without me."* The covert narcissist with whom you lived or worked wanted you weak. It was the only way they could control you. As a result, you have gotten used to living with that belief and feeling badly about yourself. When those thoughts live inside you for a long time, life feels scary and overwhelming. It feels big, while you feel small.

What would life feel like if you knew you were capable of supporting yourself? How would it feel to fully believe you are a great parent? What would it feel like to know you are really good at what you do? How would it feel to know that you will always have more than enough money? What would it be like to know you can handle anything that comes your way? What would life be like if you knew there is nothing wrong with you and so much right with you? What would it feel like to fully trust yourself?

What if you could get comfortable with being strong—with seeing yourself as a strong individual? This can be something to play with in your mind and heart. Try sitting down and asking yourself the previous questions. You will notice a feeling of peace and strength rise in you. This can be your new normal.

You are so used to feeling weak. Give yourself permission to be strong. To stand up to people. To go after what you really want. You have permission to not always be nice. Instead, be picky about who you spend your time with. Give yourself permission not to accept poor treatment anymore, from anyone.

You are allowed to fully be yourself. We need strong people with a heart like yours. Be the person you would want looking out for you.

My Story and Yours

I am someone who has experienced more than one covert narcissist, like many of you. It has changed me, too. I know this journey well.

Writing this book has changed me even more. It has awakened me to how big a problem this is worldwide, how many people are suffering because of covert narcissists. Survivors are good people.

I fell in love with everyone I interviewed. I learned so much from all of them. I also feel like I have new abilities and insights I didn't before engaging in the extensive research I did for this book. Now when I observe conversations, I recognize manipulation tactics I never would have seen through in previous years. This will happen to you, too, as you educate yourself and grow stronger. You will be amazed and empowered.

The other day, I sat with this manuscript and said, "Thank you." I didn't realize how much I personally needed this book.

I wrote every word with you in mind, dear reader. I felt a responsibility to make this truly helpful because you deserve that. We all do. I feel honored and humbled to be a part of your important healing journey. I hope it has been a help to you on your beautiful path to wholeness and freedom.

So, with that, I leave you a love letter.

Dear Survivor,

You have been through a lot, but your story is not over yet. In many ways, it is just beginning. You have a chance now. No one is controlling you anymore. You are in good hands, your hands that are full of love, authenticity, wisdom, empathy, and strength. Let your idealism, that wonderful characteristic you have, guide you and create a life that is all yours; one that reflects who you are. You get to live with you. You're very lucky.

Because of what you have been through and all the research you have done, you are developing a superpower that not everyone has. With this, you will be able to see through people faster and help people who really want and need your help. You have the capability of making this world a better place. We are lucky to have you.

Know that you are incredibly strong to have been through all you have. Know that you were targeted because of your beautiful traits, including your kind and tender heart, your nurturing spirit, and your trust of people. Please don't change these things about you because someone else was evil to you. We need people like you. The good news is now you are bringing profound wisdom to add to your tender traits. That, my dear, is an extraordinary combination.

A new world awaits you, one that is filled with people who genuinely love and respect you. A world that feels light and full of adventure.

I hope you take time to nurture yourself, to place your hand in a stream and feel the beauty that surrounds you. The quieter you get inside, through whatever helps you get there, the more you will see the richness that lies within you.

May you feel held through this tender time of healing and coming home to yourself. May you feel safe inside of you. May you come to know the truth about how valuable you are. The confusion will become clarity, the pain will turn to peace, and you will emerge with a solidness and strength that has always been there and is now ready to rise.

Take good care of yourself and know you are not alone. I, along with millions of others, am standing beside you cheering you on. We have your best interests at heart and always will.

With so much love,
Debbie

Traits of a Covert Narcissist Checklist

The DSM-IV lists traits that are used to diagnose narcissistic personality disorder. These traits manifest in different ways. The following is a list of how these are commonly exhibited in narcissists. For a more thorough examination of each of these traits and their variations, please refer to Chapter 4.

- ☐ They do not have a strong sense of self
- ☐ Silent rage
- ☐ Lying
- ☐ Hoovering
- ☐ Constant criticism
- ☐ Jealousy
- ☐ They project their own issues onto you
- ☐ Their words don't match their actions
- ☐ They are emotionally disconnected
- ☐ They have flying monkeys
- ☐ They take credit for your ideas
- ☐ They withhold praise and recognition

- ☐ They sabotage birthdays, holidays, vacations, and meaningful dates
- ☐ They belittle you and "teach you lessons"
- ☐ They are self-focused and emotionally immature
- ☐ There are always strings attached
- ☐ They use people
- ☐ They are dizzying conversationalists
- ☐ They create drama
- ☐ They don't make love; they take it
- ☐ They are not protective
- ☐ They create stories in their head
- ☐ They have no desire to know you
- ☐ They have no interest in making this a great relationship
- ☐ They use control and manipulation

Educational Resources

There is a lot of information out there about narcissism, which is helpful for you to research. You dealt with a covert narcissist, but the core traits are the same, so the information will help. Because information about the covert type takes some more digging to find, I found it helpful to read books about manipulation and control, as well, to understand what that looks like.

Books I Recommend

1. *The Wizard of Oz and Other Narcissists: Coping with the One-way Relationship in Work, Love, and Family* by Eleanor D. Payson, M.S.W.

2. *Psychopath Free: Recovering from Emotionally Abusive Relationships With Narcissists, Sociopaths, and Other Toxic People* by Jackson MacKenzie

3. *In Sheep's Clothing: Understanding and Dealing with Manipulative People* by George K. Simon, Ph.D.

4. *30 Covert Emotional Manipulation Tactics: How Manipulators Take Control In Personal Relationships* by Adelyn Birch

5. *Why Does He Do That?: Inside the Minds of Angry and Controlling Men* by Lundy Bancroft

6. *Healing from Hidden Abuse: A Journey Through the Stages of Recovery from Psychological Abuse* by Shannon Thomas LCSW

7. *Will I Ever Be Good Enough?: Healing the Daughters of Narcissistic Mothers* by Karyl McBride

8. *The Safest Place Possible: A Guide to Healing and Transformation* by Debbie Mirza (This is about healing through self-love.)

9. *The Secret Language of Your Body: The Essential Guide to Health and Wellness* by Inna Segal

YouTube is a fantastic resource. Use your own intuition as your guide as you watch. Notice how your body reacts when you listen. If you find your stomach tightening, your head feeling foggy, or your body feeling off, move to another video. Not everyone shares accurate information. Trust your body. It recognizes truth.

YouTube Channels I Recommend

1. Debbie Mirza,
   https://www.youtube.com/channel/
   UCy3cZ8214WpwqtWouiDeq-w
2. Inner Integration – Meredith Miller
   https://www.youtube.com/channel/
   UCrNg_13PdqKAZRPqyclRq1g
3. Dad Surviving Divorce (DSD)
   https://www.youtube.com/channel/
   UCUXEHz3OECVwLz1X-SNM4lw

There are many more, but these are my personal favorites.

Online Courses I Recommend

1. 6-Week Healing and Clarity After Narcissistic Abuse – https://www.debbiemirza.com/courses
2. How to Parent When Your Ex is a Covert Narcissist – https://www.debbiemirza.com/courses
3. How to Facilitate a Support Group for Survivors of Narcissistic Abuse – https://www.debbiemirza.com/courses

Helpful Websites

https://www.debbiemirza.com
http://www.kaleahlaroche.com
https://www.psychopathfree.com
https://www.wnaad.com
https//www.innerintegration.com

Articles and Videos Quoted

Jantz Ph.D., Gregory L., "What is Emotional Abuse" *Psychology Today* 12/01/2015

www.psychologytoday.com/blog/hope-relationships/201512/what-is-emotional-abuse

Mathews LPC, NCC, Andrea "When Is It Emotional Abuse" *Psychology Today* 09/26/2016

www.psychologytoday.com/blog/traversing-the-inner-terrain/201609/when-is-it-emotional-abuse

Sarkis Ph.D., Stephanie A. "11 Warning Signs of Gaslighting" *Psychology Today* 01/22/2017

https://www.psychologytoday.com/blog/here-there-and-everywhere/201701/11-warning-signs-gaslighting-in-relationships

Dr. Robert Sapolsky YouTube Video Referenced on Intermittent Reinforcement:

https://www.youtube.com/watch?v=kan2ZGqEOso

Helpful Documentary

Holy Hell: www.imdb.com/title/tt5278464

Acknowledgments

I am incredibly grateful for the people in my life who have shown me genuine love.

To my mom, for being a woman I always felt emotionally safe with. Thank you for loving me unconditionally, for giving me a foundation that has carried me through all I have experienced in this life. I miss you so much. Thank you for the woman you were, for your empathy, for your belief in me, and for your gentle spirit that held me so many times.

To Liz. I cry whenever I write about you because you mean so much to me. We have been the best of friends for so many years. You know me incredibly well. You have seen all sides of me and loved me with an unconditional love that I am incredibly grateful for. I feel the freedom to tell you anything, and that is the greatest gift. You have such a tender and genuine heart. I feel incredibly lucky and blessed to have you as my friend, my constant. You are one of my lifelines. I cherish you beyond words.

To Sonia. Thank you for being such a wonderful big sis. You and I have been through so much together, and I am so grateful to have you in my life. I love you with all my heart and strength, and anyone who gets to have you in their life is incredibly lucky and blessed.

To Cassie. I hope you always know how loved and valued you are. I hope you always live a life that is reflective of your unique and adventurous self. As you grow I want you to know my arms will always be here for you, my heart will always love you, and my eyes will always see the beauty that I have recognized in you since the day you were born. I love you so much, Cass.

To Curtis. You are such a unique and special soul. I hope you always know how worthy you are of love and respect. I hope you always trust yourself. Know that you have all the answers you need inside of you. Lucky are the people who get to be around you. I love you so deeply and am so grateful to have the honor of being your mom.

To Sonja. Thank you for being brave, for being an honest soul, and for being someone I can call at any moment and get right to things. Thank you for being someone I can trust with my heart. I am so grateful for you.

To Gary. Thank you for your steadfast encouragement with this book. Thank you for your belief in me and for all the good you bring to humanity.

To Katie. Sweet Katie. Thank you for being such a bright, shiny soul. Thank you for introducing me to hammocking and being my work buddy in the library. You are a treasure and a delight.

To John, Clyde, and Rick. You guys make me smile. Thank you for all your encouragement over the years and for your friendship. You are each so special in your own ways.

To Michelle Vandepas. You are so wonderful to work with. Thank you for all you did to get this book published and out into the world to help so many. It is a pleasure to work with you.

To Kelly Madrone. You are an amazing editor and a delightful human being! Thank you for all your hard work and your caring heart. I am so grateful for you and honored to know you.

To Michelle Morgan. You went above and beyond the call of proofreading this manuscript, and I am so grateful for you! Your eye for detail, your encouraging comments, and supportive heart was an incredible combination. Thank you!

To Camille Truman. Thank you for all you contributed to the publishing process! I always value your thoughts and expertise. You are a such a special soul, and a delight to work with.

To Meredith Miller. Thank you for writing the foreword to this book. You are such a special soul. Your tenderness and strength are stunning. The safe space you create for others is so special. Thank you for all you do to help others heal.

To the women and men I interviewed for this book. You are all amazing. You are strong and brave. Your hearts are tender and pure. This world is incredibly lucky to have you in it. Thank you. Thank you for your willingness to share your stories, for your desire to help others heal. You are an inspiration.

To the Denver and Boulder support groups. Thank you for your honesty, your vulnerability, and your strength. I have learned so much from you. I am grateful to be able to walk this road together with you.

About the Author

Debbie Mirza is a restorative coach, author, and singer/songwriter. As a coach, she works with people who are coming out of covert narcissistic relationships. She helps bring clarity and healing to survivors, providing them a safe place to be heard and validated so they can experience real love, freedom, and the strength to live a life that is in alignment with who they really are. She is also the author of *The Safest Place Possible: A Guide to Healing and Transformation.*

Learn more about Debbie's coaching practice, healing music, online courses, guided meditations, and other offerings at www.debbiemirza.com.

What Clients Say About Debbie Mirza:

"Debbie is such a bright light for victims discovering they're in an abusive relationship. After reading Debbie's book, I scheduled a few coaching calls with her that brought so much clarity and have been an anchor and reference point to me in the months since. She is well-versed in covert narcissism and gave me more insight in one session than years of therapy. As I explained a situation with my husband in which I was being blamed and feeling guilty and my belief that if I could just do more, I could fix the situation (classic narcissist behavior!), she helped me see it for what it was: blame-shifting and a tactic by him to create chaos. She then gave me such strong encouragement that I was brought to tears of relief, knowing that the strength I needed I already possessed. I am grateful for Debbie for being a beacon of light guiding victims out of the darkness."
-Cathy

"Early on in my high-conflict divorce from a covert, overt, passive-aggressive narcissist with sociopathic tendencies (whew!), a friend recommended Debbie's book. It honestly changed my life...I slurped up the audiobook like a Slurpee and immediately felt inspired and empowered. Something I had not felt in so long! I knew I needed more and went to her website and signed up for her coaching...another blessing! Debbie helped me navigate the most traumatic time of my life, where many just do not understand, to no fault of their own. Debbie is genuine and cared about me and my healing, growth, and recovery. I felt Debbie was authentically invested in me and my progress. She has given me the confidence to trust myself and the tools to recognize these toxic behaviors, signs, and characteristics. I would recommend Debbie for guidance, help, and encouragement. She is a true treasure, and she has blessed my life immensely."
-Hope

"Debbie is a light in this world who has illuminated the dark recesses of my inner world to show me where hope resides; within. I took Debbie 'within' me to explore and heal myself. With her, I was not alone. I was comforted. Safe. By selflessly sharing her experience, strength, and hope she has given me permission to do the same for myself. I am forever grateful to Debbie for having the courage to stay true to herself, in spite of fear, to be the trailblazer that she is."
-Shaleen

"Being coached by Debbie Mirza was an absolute pleasure. I had really been going through it when I found out about Debbie's book and coaching services. Coming out of an eight-year relationship with a covert narcissist, I thought I was going crazy. I just could not believe how close the things she had said in her book, and during our coaching session, was to what I had been going through in my relationship. It was almost as if she had been a fly on the wall all throughout the time I was with my ex, giving word-for-word examples and statements that were spoken to me during the relationship. To me, Debbie displayed exceptional understanding of the topic. A topic which is so greatly needed today. There are two extremes here, one in that the number of people going through this is exceptionally high, and two that the amount of information and coaches who know about this is really low. At no point during the coaching session did I feel that Debbie was doing this for financial gain, as some coaches might portray, especially if they do not have a firm grasp of the topic at hand. First, it is so hard to describe and put into words just how valuable and validating the book was. Second, the coaching provided really gave a lot of clarity to the situation I had been going through. If not for these two resources I would not be able to see myself being where I am in my current stage of healing today. I am doing great now, and Debbie was a big part of that."
-Jules